NEITHER THE ...
ANY RESPONSI...
INFORMATION CONTAINED ...
ARE STRONG AND ARE A RESULT OF THE RISE IN SOCIAL
ILLS AND THE DECLINE OF ETHICAL LIVING

Guns make men out of mice: 76

You're own code of ethics <u>truely</u> bounds you: 77-79

Faith <u>can</u> create strong morals: 61-64

Society's closeness to collapse is defined by 3 square meals: 66

Humanity's programming to accept rules + regulations and pay for "protection" from a large gang, most certainly to be concidered an organised crime sydicate: 78

Correlating and adapting the 'scope' of your dreams: 48-49

Embrace death, terror, and fear, lest you become so fearful you are scarcely alive: 60

Embrace the arts, cultural and martial, expand your mind and intellect: 19-24

Plan of action vs. state of panic. Be self-analytical practice this. p 16/69

~~religious~~ Religion reveals itself as empty, though it can bring balance and comfort: 82-83

Write your own code and <u>live</u> by it. Only then can you give an unpurposed life purpose.

Shinto? Buddhism? Asatro? ↓ as purely cultural or hereditary endeavors.

THIS BOOK IS DEDICATED TO:

THE LATE
P.O JOHNNY 'GUNS' CUMMINS

MY GRANDFATHER: A TRUE AND COURAGEOUS GENTLEMAN, A WORLD WAR II SUBMARINE VETERAN AND THE MAN WHO SHAPED A CHILD'S UNDERSTANDINGS OF THE WORLD AROUND HIM.

FEAR RULES ALL

Wordclay
1663 Liberty Drive, Suite 200
Bloomington, IN 47403
www.wordclay.com

© *Copyright 2008 Antony Cummins MA. All rights reserved.*

No part of this book may be reproduced, stored in a retrieval system, or transmitted by any means without the written permission of the author.

First published by Wordclay on 8/13/2008.
ISBN: 978-1-6048-1243-5

Printed in the United States of America.

This book is printed on acid-free paper.

SPECIAL THANKS TO:

(THE VIEWS IN THIS BOOK ARE NOT REPRESENTATIVE OF THE PEOPLE NAMED BELOW)

KATHERINE 'TUPTIM' THOMPSON: FOR SHELTERING ME THOUGH MY POVERTY SO I COULD REALIZE A DREAM.

CYNTHIA 'I JUST NEED A POOL' POWER: FOR HER INJECTION OF INSPIRATION.

PROFESSOR T INSOLL: FOR OPENING MY MIND IN WAYS YOU DO NOT REALIZE, YOU BECAME MY ACADEMIC MENTOR ABOVE ALL OTHERS.

NICK 'GYMNAST' JOHNSON: FOR THE SPELL CHECKING AND DIAGRAMS

Also by the Author

To Stand on a Stone: by Wordclay.com
To Stand On a Stone –The DVD: by How2dvd.co.uk

Eigo No Akkouzougon Jiten(A Dictionary of English Swearing)
Tokyodo publishing Japan

Author Websites

WWW.PHD-HELP.COM

WWW.ACMED-ART.CO.UK

FRONT COVER

BY

JAYSON KANE AND AUTHOR
WWW.TWOPLUSONE.CARBONMADE.COM

INTERNAL ARTWORK

BY

IOANA ATANASOVA

razpna.gfxartist.com

left@mail.bg

Conversations with an Assassin

Reflections On Modern Society

BY

Antony Cummins MA

Authors Note

I am sat in a bamboo shelter in 50 degrees of heat in the *Tongo* hills of Ghana, Africa. The *Tongo Tenzuk* people are my hosts and I am here at the pleasure of Professor T. Insoll of the University of Manchester. We are attempting to discover the archaeology and thus the history of the people of these hills. I did not start this book here and its concept was actually established a few years back, however, I am sat here writing a good section of the chapters. The first question that must be answered is: What is the purpose of this book? Its notion is strange, its category a mystery to even me. The function of this book is to make you stop and think, in that moments halt you are to look around you, look at the society we crated and realize a few things. You are to become conscious of the fact that you can make a difference to your life, you can change the way you are programmed and you can alter your own concept of existence. It is the intention of this book to help people become disciplined, to reintroduce ethics into society and to help to make people bring up their children with a higher understanding of what to teach. On the whole we want a better society but to do that we must all change a little and we must all change together, that is the point of this book.

I look at the people of the *Tongo* hills and I shudder as my concept of the 'noble savage' is destroyed. My idealistic impression of the tribes of the past is truly tested here. In this place of: alcoholism, lack of creativity, unbalanced wealth and its distribution, the sale of religion, lack of philosophy and the complete sense of strained unity. All these factors are killing my vision of how I saw the dawn of modern humans. But all hope has not been dashed, 2km down the hills we stumbled upon an Archaeological wonder, a vast expanse of iron working, pottery, lithic working and all the elements that bring together a creative people. But still the doubt lingers in my mind, as we look at trench A in the first site of the dig I see a skeleton. What was his name, was he a 'noble savage' or was he a fool, my confidence is still shaken. Out of this uncertainty is born the understanding that we have moved forward. For all the ills of modern society and its problems we are sophisticated, we are evolved but we have lost our way. We need to gain a foundation in this landside of technology. We are caught in a tidal wave that is displacing our ethics, our unity and our position in the natural world. As I watch the *Tongo* chief and his seventeen wives in' luxury' in comparison to the starving children of the tribe I wonder if we are not the same in our first world countries. We have leaders who dine on silver and people like me who can not afford to finish their education. Be it primitive ethnic groups or the high born of noble families (or political dynasties) we have lost our way as a human race. I do not dare to propose that I am changing that but what I do dare to state is that this book is a tiny step towards a better human race. If this book inspires just one future leader its purpose will have been worthy. Therefore, if you own this book, try to live by its philosophy, try to see the world we live in is a construct, it is a false world, a world that collectively we can change for the best, if we change it together.

I
Fear

The bulbous white eyes set in contrast to the shrunken grey skin of their heads, bodies in a pit decaying and pungent, each one dead, *in nomine Patris et Filii et Spiritus Sancti*. One of the dirty bodies in the stone pit moved with animation, his eyes wide and bright with life as he looked to the rim of the open funnel of his granite prison. A grimy face that was once the visage of a proud and burly combatant searched around, his scarred face covered with markings of past encounters. A naked frame shivered and looked for sanity in this hell. Days in the moss covered well that was open to the thunder green skies had left him exposed to the rain and snow, with only the bloodied black water to drink, each one of the lifeless bodies staring at the prisoner as he drank from their life-sources. Acmed the apprentice and the assassin walked over to the rim of the well, looking down at the almost spiritually crushed figure. The figure did not notice them until the assassin spoke,
"Down there, that prisoner is the apprentice to my arch nemesis, the rival assassin who would have me killed."
Acmed betrayed shock as he spoke,
"You have an enemy…another assassin, I did not know."
The assassin's voice hinted with the slightest of annoyance,
"Never show your emotions, or give away unnecessary information, never open your mind to those around you…however it matters not now, this prisoner is to die."
Acmed spoke sheepishly,
"Sorry master."

The assassin spoke without feeling but full of harsh lesson,
"What did I just tell you, don't speak with sentiment – 'sorry' is a state of emotion, you have shown that urchin down there a second flaw, take heed of my words boy."
The prisoner shouted up into the echoing night sky, teeth blood-soaked, with a hoarse tone,
"You have far to go with that one master assassin, he needs work to be done for sure."
The assassin spoke in answer,
"We all are a blank canvas at first, you too had much to learn or else you would not have been caught so easy."
The answer came,
"I would not call our struggle easy."
"Think that if you will, I say I will not argue with you, I must have respect for the dead, as you soon will be."
The prisoner in the pit showed a reflection of fear as a hunter's moon illuminated his face. The assassin turned his attention back to the apprentice stood next to him.
"Fear, fear rules everything in this life, if there was one element that was the emperor of emotions it would be fear."
Acmed the apprentice spoke with a quizzical edge to his voice,
"You mean that fear of pain and death is stronger than love or passion, a man will be more driven by fear than anything else?"
"No, that's not what I mean, but there truly is an element of truth held within what you say."

The assassin lifted an old wooden bucket, pouring its contents into the well-prison. The prisoner tried to avoid the falling rats that landed like bombs, some splashing an eruption as they hit the water, some like duds as they fell on the corpses of the dead.

"No I do not mean just physical fear of pain and death but fear in all its disguises. Of course true fear of pain is a truly persuasive force in our lives, a force that has been rendered almost null in today's society, at least for those in first world countries. True fear for your life has ended, in the modern world. How often do you see a dead body, has the average man ever seen another man killed? No, not really. Fear for your life is a dull worry that haunts you when you are caught out of familiar surroundings. No, I do not speak of just fear as you think you know it, but fear does rule our everyday lives in ways you would not think of."

Young Acmed looked into the pit where the prisoner was bravely pushing away the hungry rats, which were more then content to feast upon the dead as opposed to the living.

"You will have to do better than rats master assassin, the dead and vermin will not phase me."

The assassin smiled as he allowed the snake to slide over the edge of the well, sleek and black its silhouette held in the image of the moon.

"You just have to ask yourself is it venomous or is it a constrictor? From down there I suppose you cannot tell, and once in the water I'm sure you will not see."

The snake fell into the water like a torpedo from a tiger-moth biplane and the prisoner jumped with unease onto the pile of the dead, joining the rats' feast. The assassin turned back to his apprentice, Acmed, and continued.

"People fear all types of fear, mainly they fear loneliness, the horror of being all alone and unaccepted in this world. By nature the human mind has to find community spirit in some fashion, even in this modern world with its individualistic format and nuclear families we join groups for the feeling of belonging. Sports teams with colours and flags, clubs and activity groups, all of them houses for those who fear to be alone. A small percentage of the people involved in them will actually have a true passion for the focus of the clubs attention, a true love of the team or activity they do. The rest persuade themselves of a love for the group focus because the feeling of belonging is addictive. You can easily test this by the fact that most people love the sports team of their town, if it was a certain team that they fell in love with then people would automatically move to a different town and not simply support the team closest to them. It is the infrastructure of love and social networking that they adore, they have a fear of being alone not a love for the 'spoke' that keeps the group functioning."

Down in the well the black serpent had climbed the hillock of carcasses, its starved condition searching for the platter of vermin that waited unknowing. The prisoner leaped upon it and muttered under strain,

"Constrictor."

Acmed looked into the well as the assassin continued with unwavering calm.

"If you can think of it men fear it; loneliness, to be unloved, death, pain, humiliation, anything, there is always a constant fear that exists in men's hearts and minds. What you have to do, young apprentice, is understand that. Understand that in your conscious mind you live a story of your life, not what your true life is but what you think it is. In there, in this story, you try to beat the fear by romanticising. What you must do is analyse each section of your life with a four-step process. You must, separate the truth from the fiction in your mind, pinpoint what it is you fear about that situation, then rationalise your fear and understand that it is this fear that is driving you to a decision. Once you have understood the truth of the situation choose the best option, knowing that fear is there but not affecting your choice."

1) SEPARATE THE TRUTH FROM FICTION

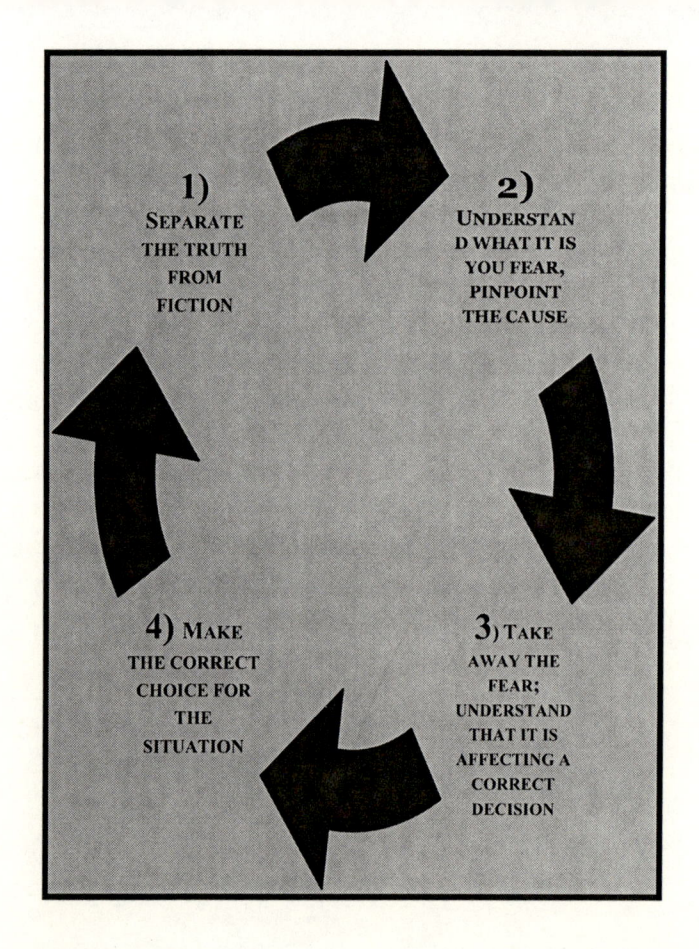

2) UNDERSTAND WHAT IT IS YOU FEAR, PINPOINT THE CAUSE

3) TAKE AWAY THE FEAR; UNDERSTAND THAT IT IS AFFECTING A CORRECT DECISION

4) MAKE THE CORRECT CHOICE FOR THE SITUATION

The prisoner in the well snapped the neck of the snake; its black body limp in the mire beneath. He shouted up, an edge of triumph with a hint of anticipation in his voice.
"Come on master assassin, what are you waiting for, kill me, this torture is disrespectful to our class, and we each deserve a quick death, a professional courtesy."
The assassin looked into the pit, a wry smile, then humility came over him.

"You will have to forgive me. Even though you are the protégé of my enemy you are correct, politeness does dictate that I should kill you now. However, the lesson to my apprentice outweighs the need for courtesy, and as you know a true human mind is priceless, so please accept my forgiveness."

The prisoner started to lose his cool and search the well for hand holds as the assassin turned back to Acmed.

"You see Acmed, cool and reserve are the true characteristics of a human. Animals and beasts panic, the divine gift of self sacrifice and reserve in hostile situations is one of man's most fabulous tools."

Acmed responded with a tone that started to show the self-organising of his mind,

"So, you are saying that we should understand fear, understand what it does to our rational thought, isolate it and then accept the consequences of the situation we are in."

The assassin inserted,

"Yes that's true, but you must analyse all possibilities first. Never just throw your life away, but if you know in all honesty that the situation has no solution then be reserved, show a stiff upper lip and take it like a gentleman…now lets put it to the test."

The assassin lifted a bucket up to the well edge; a bucket with a hidden content, hidden by a towel that lay on top. The prisoner looked up to the edge and beheld a towel fall from a bucket and the contents rain down. It was here at this moment a thousand years flashed past his eyes, an eternity of thought voyaged across his mind in an instant. The prisoner looked to every possibility and to all solutions, panic

crossed his face for but a second, and then like a serene being it left him and the snakes fell into the water, splashing to the sound of the master assassins voice,
"They are not constrictors."
The assassin turned to Acmed and smiled,
"His was a good end, a true human, remember Acmed…Fear is the mind killer."

II
ART

"Master, I don't fully understand, why are we doing this? Don't get me wrong I appreciate the beauty of the project but you said today was a lesson to be aware of."

Acmed put down his paintbrush and lifted his face to the sunlight coming through the roof windows to the Masters studio.

"You mean what has this got to do with the Marital Arts, assassination and the connecting subjects that will make you a more advanced tactician and killer?"

The master assassin continued to apply his brush stroke as he answered the student with a dry tone as Acmed slumped back in his chair and answered back,

"Yes, something like that. I mean I can paint to a certain level and I don't mind it as a relaxation aid but I'm on tenterhooks waiting for the lesson."

"What makes you think that this is not the lesson?"

The assassin looked semi-unimpressed with his last stroke on the canvas, waiting for the students reply.

"Because there is no political aim to the conversation, usually our lessons revolve around the political, the martial or the reflective."

The assassin concentrated on correcting his mistake,

"When I was a young apprentice assassin like yourself, I concentrated on mainly the Martial Arts, I would travel the world, search out the next master to learn from, I would comb the earth for master martial artists. Then one day an old master of mine, a man called Dennis, a true powerhouse of destruction, sat with me for a day in Japan. We were there training with a Ninjutsu master. When he sat me down he showed me his drawings and expressions of the Martial Arts. He told me then that when you climb up the ladder of mastery it is like standing on a stone above a crowd. It is a struggle climbing on to the stone, it takes you a long time but once you are up there you are separated from the riff raff beneath you. When you look to the horizon you realise that there are others at periods also stood on rocks, they too have mastered the arts and they stand above the crowd. You see Acmed in reality what he was saying is that you can tell a master by the way they walk, the way they hold themselves, the way they behave in a crowd. He said it is almost like they were stood up on a rock, they stood out so much. But what I did not realise was that he was talking about a master of any art; dancing, painting, poetry and any other art you can think of. If you master a creative art you will put your mind in a state of purity, whilst indulging in your chosen art you will be working with the subconscious and allowing enlightenment to creep into your veins."

Acmed responded,

"So you are saying that by painting I can become a better martial artist and a better human?"

"That is so, you can. Most people whittle away the hours of their lives with distractions, light entertainment that nullifies the boredom and stimulates the mind to a minimum, just allowing pleasure to creep around the edges of their state of being. When they try to indulge in something more creative then what they can usually achieve they hit a wall, this wall is the wall of beginning, a structure that is there because your subconscious cannot understand the patterns that your body wishes to move in. Because this wall is here and they do not have the vision to surmount the wall and train the subconscious to enjoy the challenge and to learn the movements they resort back to the quick fix of the light stimulation. Many times throughout their lives they will become bored with this stimulation and they will again try something from the vast category of arts that are out there. But again the wall of beginning will hit them and again they will retreat to their comfort of spiritual hibernation. But when you learn that the pleasure is in defeating the wall and allowing your body and mind to push forward and create, then there is true joy in the hearts of men, joy that cannot be bought. I have seen some of my previous students filled with joy at a painting that they have done. In all honesty the painting was terrible; if it was reviewed it would be established to be worthless. However, the artist who painted it can spend hours looking at his own image, as to him it is pure beauty; it represents a vision past the wall in our minds. But what do you think he achieved in that terrible painting?"

The assassin sat back with a smile as he had corrected his mistake and Acmed put down his brush with frustration and spoke with an annoyed tone,

"He achieved a goal, his mind had set itself a goal and he saw a point of accomplishment and surpassed it, giving a deeper feeling of satisfaction then the light entertainment could provide."

The assassin swished his paint as he mixed it,

"You are correct of course, but what else did he do? Well he sat in silent contemplation for a period of maybe six hours whilst doing this. How often do people sit in silent contemplation for six hours? Not often I can tell you that. Silent contemplation during painting is the same as meditation, when you are in the true 'zone of painting' you are working from a subconscious level, you are creating movement from your body through images from your mind, you are not thinking in a language, you are thinking in pictures. This free flowing movement quietens your mind and allows you to enter an animal state, the state of reacting with your environment. After this 'meditation' has happened on a regular occurrence you find it easy to transcribe that feeling from your time at the easel to other situations. Your shoulders drop, the tension leaves you and you can go into a meditative trance easier as you have spent hours in that state of mind. Painting and art truly help you become a master assassin, they allow you to start your path to master level, and it gives you the deep understanding of the stillness of life and allows your eyes to take on that glow, the one filled with the divine spark."

The assassin sat back and looked at his creation on the canvas with a smile before he continued,

"Music has the same focus, music comes from the heart, at first learning to play an instrument is torture, the unfamiliar finger positions and strange arrangements of your body urge you to give in. But like art, once you hit that zone you never realise you are there, you also exist in the moment. In total what I am saying young Acmed, is that to become a master in anything, no matter what, as long as it has root in the subconscious when you are proficient, will further your path as a human and an assassin. The painter can see and reason with the dancer and the musician; the racing car driver can feel the same as the chess player. You can use the lessons of the world across the board of your life, allowing yourself to become a fuller person, quieter, more sensitive, mentally aware and filled with divine light, a true human. Throw away your TV and learn something, in today's world we see anything that has no function in the production of money or the acquirement of materialistic as useless. This is a lie. Cover your basic needs and then dispose of monetary adventures. Learn the things that encourage beauty of the spirit and support you as a fully constructive being. Life is beautiful and sometimes true mastery of your own art comes from seeking mastery in another's arena."

Acmed picked up his brush and started to paint again, this time just letting flow the strokes from his mind.

"I understand you mainly, but how can I try to stop the strokes being conscious efforts, I need to think where the brush should go."

The assassin sat forward with animated enthusiasm,

"This is the hardest part, at first of course you have to think with the conscious mind, but it is constant practice that allows your body to know where the brush should go and what pressure to apply. Just concentrate on moving your body and mind with flow, but just keep practicing. Eventually your body will start to take over, then you will find that the paint flows on to the canvas, and from that your knife will find the correct spots and your body will evade any threats, just let go by constant meditation with a strive to reprogram your body, throw away what the modern world has taught you. The behaviour becomes learnt and automatic, the naturalistic trance state is enhanced and can then be developed and matured."

Acmed stood up and breathed in the morning air, stood back and looked at his painting. It wasn't much better, but there was something different about it now. Then he realised he had been concentrating on the conversation whist he painted, and it seemed he had improved.

III
NOBILITY

"Do you think Raymond Lull would be happy with the state of nobility and the aristocratic class at the minute?"

The two assassins, teacher and pupil, sat under a gnarled oak tree in the dying light of the castle grounds.

"What do you mean master? I know of Raymond Lull and his early writings[1] on chivalry, but what has that to do with monarchs and the nobility of the day, except for the connections with rank?"

The assassin looked to the early evening moon and the setting sun as he spoke, legs crossed,

"What does it mean to be noble? Master Lull gives it in full detail and the origins of such according to him. He states that in the beginning the greater men surfaced from those around them, rising to power, champions among men, the cream of the crop. It was these people, who took to arms, protected the populace and led them in wise counsel. But I tell you this young one, I have thought for a long time, where did the change come? Which part of history did these men live in, when there was the possibility of leadership without corruption? Was it the Vikings? After reading the sagas I would say no. Was it the early Anglo-Saxons? The Celts we have no real idea about or at least not enough to answer that question. The Romans we know to be completely corrupt and

---

[1] Book of Knighthood and Chivalry: Raymond Lull – Chivalry Bookshelf

their power misused. Of course in each geographical location the time of the insertion of dishonesty must have been different, but for us here in the west when was it? When did it change from the populace being of basic equality and looking to the proficiently minded, to the small step of corruption where that person in position misused their power? Even for something as simple as starting to ask for menial tasks to be done for them instead of doing it themselves, thus putting the work under them and indirectly stating that they are too good to be doing such things. Leaving the conclusion that that person who has been assigned the task to be of lower status then them, this I think is where it all began."

Acmed pulled his scarf around his neck and ventured, "Maybe corruption has always been there?"

The assassin gave a smile and nodded,

"I don't doubt that corruption has probably been there since the beginning of time, but what I want to know is, where was the point that corruption took hold of power and when things that were obviously corrupt and non-practical came into play? Where was the point when the change came from a leader giving an idea that was generally accepted as bad and someone piping up and saying 'no you are wrong', to the point where the bad plan or command is given and people accepted this and then behind closed doors professed how terrible an action it would be? This is the point in history I want to find because this was the start of the corruption of nobility, the miniscule starting point that ended in the Egyptian definition of the pharaoh being a living god; Greek leaders the descendents of gods; roman emperors gods for the day, and the kings of England and Europe being so proclaimed rightful heirs by divine command. This is the point I have struggled to find, it is most disagreeable."

Before Acmed could interact more in this conversation the assassin continued, calm as ever,

"Can you image if one of the monarchs of England followed the same path as the Roman Emperor *Licinius?*"

Acmed turned his head in question,

"Who is *Licinius?*"

"He was an emperor that came from the peasant class; he rose through the system and came to power. Can you imagine coming from 'humble' birth and dieing as a god? Incredible!"

Acmed quizzed, pushing his scarf back again,

"So, where have your studies brought you to, what is the point in history that you have come to, when was the start of corruption?"

The assassin uncrosses his legs and looked to the sky, the blanket of the heavens covering the castle and the tree,

"I postulate that it must be at the same point as the human race changes from Mesolithic to Neolithic, hunter gatherer to agriculture, I feel that it was here, when wealth could be accumulated, when a power base was established. Before that bad leadership could result in the death of the tribe, the clan could be led astray, but with the surplus of crops and the easier living of the Neolithic bad leadership could prosper. I'm not saying that they had tyrants like the Romans and the post-renaissance monarchs of Europe but the seeds of fraud were sown in the establishment of hereditary governorship."

Acmed challenged the master
"So, what do you think of the modern monarchy, modern rulership."
The assassin smiled and looked to his apprentice,
"The modern nobility, that's a strange affair, and I don't just mean nobles by birth. Alongside the still reigning monarchs I include Prime Ministers, Presidents and governors. The fundamental fault with this type of rule is that it is hereditary and its establishment is based on the luck of the draw whilst in the womb, not exactly the correct basis for distribution of power. I understand and can sympathise with why the hereditary system was established. It's true that, a father or mother and the surroundings can shape the child, from a dreadful family you will probably get a bad child and from a high-quality family you will get a good child. Of course the nature/nurture argument is huge and some examples of the opposite of a parent coming in its offspring is true, just look to the legend of *Mordred*. But society has forgotten the magic of chivalry and of good-blood, in fact as time goes on good-blood is dying and nurture is taking over the nature of things and we are living in a world of demons."
Acmed looked to his master,
"Do you really have such little faith in humanity?"
The assassin replied,
"I have faith that the seeds for a better life are within the ground, beneath the social structure we have but on the whole I feel there is worse to come before it gets better."
The assassin continued,

"The fact that a queen is a queen and a king is a king is no longer the fact of quality surfacing, but due to tradition we owe them leadership. Even the American Presidents are becoming a heredity faction, both fathers and sons coming to power and Acmed do you think they have risen to the heights of power by merit and guile? No, of course not. They have come from powerful families that have established themselves through wealth. The world is laughing at their ridiculous rule, the entire world. Their decisions do not benefit the people, quite the opposite. Do you want to know what I think? I think that most of the monarchs, leaders and governors of the world have ancestors of quality. They were the nobles of their time, true kings, but the distinction between noble and peasant became stronger, the intermarriages between the two drifted and eventually diminished and became outlawed. Thus the peasants could breed and share genes and a tough life killed off the weak. Whereas the nobility began to inbreed, only staying within strict family limits, creating weak individuals and leaving the tell tale signs of a few genes to select from. How many of the nobility seeded slave girls in the past, pushing the good genes back into the populace and legitimising inbred heirs with other noble houses. A thousand years this process has gone on for. If you think about it, the strong minded and the physically fine genes exist in sections of the peasant class, they have become the strongest and have the 'good-blood'. They have the argument of nature on their side but now with our social system the argument of nurture is too strong, there will have to be revolution in some parts of the world."

Acmed posed the question,
"Are you anti-royalist?"
The assassin turned with pride,
"God no, I am a royalist through and through – I truly believe in the right to rule by a monarch, if it was up to me I would tear down the government and place a monarch in complete command. With today's technology and the speed of information a tyrant could not rule, they would be disposed in some way. What we need is a new system and a reshuffle of the aristocracy, and for those countries who don't think they have an aristocracy and are all equal, places like America, they should look again. The definition of aristocracy is a powerful ruling family, and what are their top presidential families if not that.

Acmed interrupted, "Here comes the target."
"Get into position." came the command.
The man came walking along the footpath strolling on his own, a rump and red nosed creature, fat with indulgence. Acmed shouted over,
"Can you help me sir, my daughter is stuck up in the hollow of this old tree."
The man looked over and raised his hand, his direction changed and he walked over to help, speaking as he approached,
"Stuck in a hollow, eh? There were the days when I could climb a hollow, now I would have trouble getting in."
Acmed replied,
"Thanks for your help, I can't get her down."
Then from the hollow of the tree came the cries of a meek young girl 'Help me... I'm stuck!' surrounded by blubbering. The man looked inside the giant

hollow of the gnarled oak tree and he heard the click of a tape recorder and the crying stopped.
"What is this, who are you people?" the man questioned with haste,
A fumble ensued, the crunching of bones and the churning of blood came from the hollow and the assassin emerged with blood-soaked clothes and a white-toothed grimace.
"Sometimes you just have to get bloody to change things."

IV
THE CASTE SYSTEM

The rust covered iron ball crunched against the remains of the 'factory orange' brick wall. Another success for the crane driver and his mission of annihilation on this edifice graveyard, this building site full of its yellow reflective jacket army, each one bent on the destruction of the once proud building. Within the middle of this construction site were two figures dressed in work attire, shovelling stone, worker ants for the hellish overseer, whose demonic eyes searched from his cabin, overlooking his minions, finding fault and waiting to dish out a verbal onslaught to his subjects, a bloody monarch of a destroyed kingdom. The two shovelling new workers progressed at a steady pace as they conversed with each other.

"Is this a good spot for surveillance my young apprentice?" the assassin spoke as he shovelled stone from a pile into a wheelbarrow.
"It is indeed, we can see the target, we have the contract, and we have reason and access to the kill." responded Acmed, the ever faithful student.
The assassin looked with a kindness in his eyes upon his protégé, a rare smile as the trainee had his head bent down for work.
Acmed lent on his shovel,
"Look at these men, they are zombies, just working without love of anything, waiting for the shift whistle to end there suffering."
The assassin lent on his shovel too and joined the conversation.
"You see Acmed, these people have been ripped out of the caste system, they have been torn from their

natural environment and forced into slavery for fat bosses just like him in the cabin over there."

Acmed quizzed at the caste system remark.

"Are you talking about the predominantly Hindu endogamous hereditary groups of India? If memory serves me they are called groups often termed as *jātis*."

The proud assassin responded with hidden love,

"Educated as ever, you could say that, but again that is a dogmatization of the reality of true caste systems. You see the caste system is a natural development of real humans."

"What do you mean by real humans?"

The assassin pondered with his eyes,

"I mean a human that has no social restrictions put upon him, a human that is born into a free world where land is plentiful and government systems are few, a land where your choice of path is not governed for you by the luck of where you are born. For instance, if you were born into an upper middle class family here in England you would have university education and go on to choose from one of the vocational professions; dentist, lawyer, and other such things. Where as if you were born in Mongolia on the steppes you would not have the option of being a dentist but instead have the option of being predominantly a herdsman, do you follow me?"

The apprentice questioned back with finger talking alongside his mouth,

"Therefore, if the upper-middle class lawyer wanted to be a herdsman he would find it most difficult to enter that profession and equally the herdsman would not have the chance of becoming a lawyer, they are thrown into the limited professions that are available to them."

The assassin broke in,

"Yes that is it, but people will automatically side with the lawyer having the best profession. But what if in that lawyer's heart he wanted nothing more then to feel the wind on his face, ride with a clan and have the happiness of freedom, what if money was not his goal, then he is doomed to a life of stagnant existence and wishing, until one day he becomes the zombie, the social construct that is made everyday by modern society. Ninety percent of the world's population are zombies to their forced caste, forced into a class system that they did not choose, into a society that demands money from them and only allows them to live if they follow within the thin limitations of that government, forcing the free spirit of a human to exist in a nightmare world, a world that defeats them and zombifies their mind, ruining a truly magnificent creature."

The overseer jumped from his cabin, concrete covered and fuming with diabolical stare, spittle erupting like demonic flame as his anger thrust itself through the air to the assassin and his apprentice.

"You two lazy bastards, you have been on my books now for two weeks, two weeks and you work like nattering women, constantly talking, a mothers' meeting indeed, get on with your work or ship out you daft bastards."

With the onslaught over, the cabin door slammed shut as the supervisor's eyes looked out through the dark window of his office, a gleaming Balrog in the depths. The assassin and the apprentice feigned shock and carried on with their work, shovelling and shovelling as the everlasting loads came and came again but this time they spoke as they worked.

"You see young one, in the beginning before social oppression there were a few castes or roles played out by traditional peoples that naturally evolved as needed depending on the environment that they lived in:

1. The leaders or council of wisdom
2. Knowledge seekers
3. The hunters, gatherers, farmers and producers of food
4. The cooks and those for food preparation
5. Healers and doctors
6. Warriors and fighters
7. Construction
8. Artists, poets and storytellers alongside historians
9. Craftsmen
10. Outcastes in the true sense of the word, people who could not fit into a mutually beneficial society, thieves and murderers.

Don't be fooled my young apprentice, we are outcastes in the true sense of the word, we do not belong in society, that is why we live outside of its rules, we are true outcastes and we will die unloved and hated."

The apprentice put down his shovel and placed his fingers over his mouth,

"You are saying that from these original 'castes' in life we have spawned all of the others?"

The assassin joined him in a moment's relaxation,

"Yes Acmed, that's correct. From my list sprang all the other professions and services needed for society to evolve. In the beginning, the very beginning each one was all of the above, he had to be part leader, part construction and so on as the tribes were so small that knowledge in all areas was needed. But as numbers grew the need for specialisation came. This is the height and the golden era of the caste system, for it was here when the best person for the job came forth, when the most skilled and able was to do the work needed. Each person could create and add to the clan, did you know that Neanderthals could make a blade that was monomolecular all the way around its edge, monomolecular, now do you think every single Neanderthal could do that? No of course not, a few members of the tribe would be able to do that, that was their natural skill, their calling. However as society grew and grew and social classes became prevalent and access to follow your own caste calling became more difficult, as machines took over jobs, artisans were no longer needed, only mechanics to look after the machines. Think before the industrial revolution, every single thing was handmade, everything, from clothes to boxes to knives, all of it, then like thunder came the machines and the artisan dies overnight. A massive percentage of the population is redundant, their natural calling taken over by mindless machines. So what do they do now?

They find another gap in the employment sector, anything to cover the rent and feed the children. Why hand-craft something when no one will buy it or pay the deserving amount for it? Look around you now, look around at these workers, how many are painters in their spare time, how many are dreaming of the workshop they have at home and the woodcraft they do as a hobby, or are building models of their favourite things? Are these idle time fillers or their true caste calling trying to free itself from a dogmatized world? Ask your self this Acmed, how many warriors do you see here?"

The apprentice looked to the ranks of zombies as they worked too, he automatically chose a few hard faced workers and pointed them out and said,

"Those, but they are too fat, they are grotesque."

The assassin answered with a quick whit,

"Fat indeed, but only fat through failure and ease of lifestyle, even though they are construction workers the machines do their bidding and they eat as though they are working. But you are correct, they are the warriors. Think now how the military has changed. It does not want many fighters, only a hand full for the front line; it does not search for leaders in the officer ranks. It searches for mathematicians, linguists and hypothesis creators, modern weapons do the work, warriors are no longer needed on such demand anymore. Think of these people here, some of them would excel in a Viking shield wall, a roman *Testudo* formation or as Mongolian horsemen, Celtic warlords or berserkers. That is were they should be, not shoveling stone and concrete, but their skills are not needed, the warriors of today are not warriors but from other castes, leaving only what society has for them, eventually turning them into fat zombies and slaves until death, spirits killed by out casting them."

The devil appeared, Baphomet in flames, an aging, deformed cherub at the cabin door.
"That's the final straw! You two lazy good-for-nothings in my cabin when the shift ends, get your arses into my office when the whistle blows!"

The assassin and apprentice looked to each other with a knowing look and replied in unison,
"Aye, sir."
They picked up their shovels and carried on working.
The assassin gave a muffled whisper,
"Remember though apprentice, every one has a little selection of each caste in them, even the warrior can paint to some extent and the cook can sing or write a poem, its not a case of you have a natural caste and that's it, you simply have talents in a predominant area. The key to life is to become proficient in all things, a master of all. But in this world with modern society there is no chance for blooming, it's just a network of zombie factories churning out blasphemous images under God."

With that the whistle blew and the workmen stopped, another day of toil finished, another day's rent and food on the table, men could now return to their 'hobbies'. The assassin and apprentice entered the gate to Hades as they climbed the cabin stairs, they opened the door to reveal the master, enthroned upon a tattered mount and surrounded by bland oil stained calendars and pornography. The stale smell of bacon sandwiches held the air and his face grew dark and sinister. The manager shot out of his seat, mouth open about to spew forth his argument, when Acmed pulled a blade from his boot and slipped it with ease into the foreman's mastoid gland. The assassin was on him like a fox, a garrotte around his neck and the hideous face of the overseer found a new level of unsightliness. His life ended in putrid filth, a zombie of the highest extreme and outcast of the highest order.

Acmed spoke to the assassin,
"Target dead, area secure, witnesses nil"
The assassin responded
"Death confirmed, target has found his calling in life, a victim of us outcastes"
They both smiled with a strange wickedness.

V
MODERN WARFARE

The dark chocolate wood of the museum gave it authority and power, a transmitter of knowledge and lessons. The assassin looked down into the glass case at the ivory covered crossbow, a marvellous blend of cream and brandy held together with cold black iron.
"That there is the end of the world, a true feature of Armageddon, the destroyer of social order and the last breath of the human race."
The apprentice shrugged his shoulders and spoke with a searching intelligence,
"I can think of a few more weapons that have caused more pain and death than the crossbow."
The master assassin looked to him with a fatherly smile,
"Go on, which weapons?"
The response came quick and liner in tone,
"Atomic weapons, grenades, land mines, torpedoes and of course the gun."
The assassin gave a look of enlightenment,
"Ah yes, the gun...and what pray-tell is the gun?"
The answer came with minimum waiting and with academic regurgitation,
"A mechanical system that fires a projectile via the release of a trigger mechanism..."
The apprentice's words trailed of as his finished the sentence and looked with a smiling recognition to his master.
"Exactly young one, yes the cross bow is a gun...of sorts but still a gun by definition and it is with this simple trigger mechanism here that the world was

changed forever, it would take the collapse of all society and industry to unlearn that little secret, a secret that will take mankind to the grave."

The assassin continued with his theory lesson to a more keen, eager student,

"Have you seen the Rambo films?"

"Yes I have seen them master, they have their place."

"But did you see the last one made, the 2008 film?"

"I did master, I saw that too."

The assassin satisfied with his inquiry continued,

"Well put yourself into your mind and imagine the situation."

The apprentice assassin closed his eyes and rested his hand on the viewing cabinet as the image unfolded in his mind.

"You are in a conflict country of south East Asia, the woodland around you is green and dark, mist on the ground. The village is in front of you, traditional and quiet; women tend to babies, men, slim, athletic, cut at branches and go about their farming and business of construction or fishing. Then in these relative peace comes the first explosion, a rain of hell-flame appears from nowhere. Then you see them, Hades-spawn, rushing from the foliage, green suited and carrying the demon weapon, the gun. They run from hut to hut, there is no mercy, just bodies erupting from the inside as gunfire tears life asunder. Those who can flee try and find shadows of lead block their path. The butchery of the rebellious village males is instantaneous and without decision. Children are smashed under boot and boys beaten to the floor and once the men have all been killed with minimum effort the rape begins. Rape on a massive scale, girls, children, boys, the old, then comes pillage, slavery and burning. The raid is complete, one sided and quick, life destroyed in one."

The assassin's quiet voice trailed off but before the apprentice could open his eyes or comment the master assassin continued.

"Now picture yourself back to the village just before the attack, back to the fishing and the tending of the young. You are there watching as there is a massive roar from the woods, men run from the bushes, this time they are holding machetes, knives, spears and rocks. The women scream, the babies cry as they come rushing in. The first wave of village men are killed or wounded upon the fury of the raiders. A section of the raiders don't seem to be attacking, they are running straight for the loot, a few are capturing women in this short time of reprieve. Then it comes, the men of the village run from the rivers edge and from the fields. They two have knives and blades in hand, they form into a group and run to the centre of the village to match the raiders. The two sides clash in the centre, blood flies, cries of the dying sound in Eden. After a few minutes a raider gives out the sign and they all retreat back into the forest, they retreat with a few women and some goods, casualties are had on both sides."

The assassin paused and the apprentice opened his eyes,

"You see my young student, while the second description still holds the terror and hell of the first the second is the natural order of the world, in the 21st century we all try to believe that the world can exist in harmony, while there are too many people on this earth that will never be, war is to man as hunting is to the shark, inescapable. The second version is acceptable to the human heart; we can accept this smaller evil as we can defend against it. We can train and plan against a reality that cannot be avoided. The first one however is much different. This is an evil we can not live with, this is unmatchable to the victims, there is no defence, no reprieve just anarchy and chaos and chaos is what the human mind can not comprehend – a life without hope is a dead human from the inside. I would prefer to be a corpse with a grin and a dying light in the eyes then an empty human walking in a world of fear, a world that should never have existed, a world that came from the invention of that trigger there in the cabinet before you."

The apprentice looked at the beautiful weapon before him.

"Who would think such anarchy could come from such a simple thing…a trigger?"

The master assassin changed direction in his conversation,

"In that forest that I made you imagine did you see any industrial factories?"

Acmed looked up from the weapon to his master,

"No."

"Of course you didn't, but guns have to be made somewhere in some industrial environment. They don't just grow on trees, somebody somewhere knows where they come from and that somebody is modern and has the ethics of a modern society. You see in the west we have developed the gun, it took hundreds of years for it to enter our world as we see it now and over those centuries we have put ethics upon it. We could fill our streets with guns but the general populace would not be inclined to raid the high street and take slaves, and butcher people. Look at America, they have massive amounts of gun violence and problems but even they don't do what happens in traditional nations when the gun is thrust upon them. In America gun violence is usually between rival gangs, I'm sure if all the people of America got together and joined forces it would be the biggest already armed unit in the world. But even they are not that mad and why? It's because the gun has evolved in their ethos, their subconscious understands that it would be detrimental to their own society to take such a path. For those for whom the gun is relatively new, the gun is a disease spreading through them, killing the population, a true evil. If the devil exists today he is in league with the arms dealers and their trade, may they be cursed in hell for eternity."

The apprentice looked upon the cross bow,

"What about modern weapons and warfare in the first world countries?"

The assassin smiled,

"I feel that has found its natural balance, an evil that also should not exist but does, heaven thank that it appears to be level headed, as the major nations of the world have found equilibrium. An equilibrium, that is only occasionally broken by stupid leaders and for reasons of power and money. We humans have seen much modern warfare and it is true it is not needed, but at least we try to keep it military and not a civilian matter, well some of us anyway. If you think about it Acmed the armament of modern weapons has been invented, its there and that's a fact. However, it is also a fact that we have enough weapons to destroy the planet many times over, enough chemicals to destroy the plants of the planet, enough weapons to put a gun in the hands of most men of this world and enough weapons to raise an army bred for the extinction of man. We have all of this but still we stand here in a world of relative peace, with war breaking out at its seams only relatively occasionally. It is a tribute to man that we can hold it together and live in basic unity whist we have the capability to play god and begin the *Ragnorock*, the Viking version of hell on earth and the end of man. Its true I wish for the world to return to the sword where one man can outdo another and romance and adventure is born out of horror, born because there is hope, but in this world where we cannot change reality and un-invent the gun, we are doing well enough to give tribute to the humanity still held in mankind."

VI
SPACE

Acmed looked through the spotting telescope and the assassin looked down his rifle's magnified scope, both looking at the same target both looking through cross-hairs. The man in their vision was sitting at an office desk, tie and shirt undone, window closed to the night air and an orange glow spilling into the streets. The man was on the phone, shouting, holding his hair, loosening his tie more, his fan was on but the night was not warm, his warmth came from frustration. The two hawks of the night watched as he strode about, telephone in hand. What this man could not have known is that these two eavesdroppers were listening to his every word, waiting for a codeword to be said by this frustrated man's telephone partner, a partner that had hired a hit if problems of the past were not resolved.
"Do you think he is losing his control?"
Acmed smirked as he said the words and the assassin spoke back with quiet restraint, not at Acmed's interruption but simply because that was his way.
"I think he's lost it entirely. Its only through a last ditched effort that he is trying to pull himself back in the clear. He has broken down and his only salvation is to let his body talk whilst his mind races for answers, I wonder if he knows, if he feels he is on the edge of death?"
Acmed nodded as he agreed with the master assassin, then uncharacteristically the assassin looked at his apprentice and asked,

"What do you do when you are stressed beyond belief, what are your thoughts on that matter?"

Acmed looks at the assassin with a slight sideward's glance as this was quite unusual, the assassin was always 100% for the job, this conversation with an assassin was most irregular. However, with precaution Acmed began his monologue.

"What do I do? Well I think of space."

The assassin looked from his sights,

"Good choice, why?"

Acmed responded with a patronised glare,

"You know why."

"Indulge me."

So the apprentice continued with sluggishness at first, "When we look inward at the earth and we make our world smaller, we confine ourselves to the belief that our problems are important. What people don't realise about problems is that problems are self-made. The only true problems in life are finding food, keeping warm and staying safe. Any other problem in life is not actually a problem; it's an inconvenience or a self-imposed target that you are not reaching. For example the writer who wishes to be an author, or the boy who wants to be an officer in the navy, the man who wants to have a better home. These things are all self-targets that sometimes you miss. However, these 'problems' become confines for your mind. The hermit who has chosen to leave behind the material world has sliced the rope of target away from himself, he does not need the better car, better house, more expensive jewellery, he simply deals with the core problems of living, once you have those sorted out you have a happy life. The problem is, instead of looking on an insular spectrum you are best looking to the outer realms, things that are beyond you. Most people concentrate on the microcosm as opposed to the macrocosm. When I look into space and I'm not just talking of at night when the city light pollution allows, I'm also talking of reading books and watching documentaries on the subject, I find my 'problems' shrink. When you realise that the scope of your dreams are miniscule in comparison to the reality of the world you live in, life becomes sweeter."

The assassin took his eye away from the scope again and spoke with that monotone voice,

"Do you think our target down there can see space from his window?"

Acmed, with an equally monotone voice spoke back,

"He would not see space if it fell from the sky and engulfed him. All his life he has looked to himself, look at his watch, look at his furnishings, these are not the elements of a man of open-mindedness, these are the fruits of a tunnel vision person. He has forsaken the true beauty of the universe and trapped himself in a prison of expectation."

Acmed looked to the sky and then talked more with somewhat excited animation,

"What he should do is take a good look at his life and concentrate on what is truly important to him. Right now he is living his life, but he is actually thinking purely of the future and forgetting that he is in fact experiencing the now, his goals have trapped him in a search for a better living, but there is no end result to this journey, he does not realise that he is chasing his tail, he will work for more materialistic value and then when he has achieved his goal and his problems are solved, he will instigate a new set of targets and trap himself in a prison again, its madness."

The man in the window pulled the phone away from his ear in anger and, sore without sound, put the phone back to his ear after this reprieve and started again,

"We should just kill him now and go home, I think he is in too deep to get out."

Acmed spoke and yawned in the cool night,

"Master, what do you do when you have such problems...if you have them that is?"

"Of course I have them, I am human; however young one, I can safely say that I have kept my targets within reach of my abilities and therefore have no need to look too far outwards to regain control of my life. But if I do need to I look to history, to the past to the deeds and lives of others, to see that we are all mortal and that I shall soon be festering in a sweet grave alongside them. This brings me 'back to Earth' and makes me think of the reality of the universe that we live in and the reality of the problems I don't have."

The assassin paused then continued,

"This guy here, he has the answer to everything at his disposal, the problem he has is that he is about to die, why? For money and power. If he gave up that money and gave up that power then he would not die, but his need to fulfil his target is so strong that he has forgot the type of man that he is dealing with and in what manner he got his power and money. If he just let go of it all he would have no problems, he has enough personal money to live, what more could he

want that is worth his life. He is blind to the reality of the universe he has created for himself. We are all born into the different situations that we are given, some are tougher than others, some come with too much stress but on the whole it is your decision to eliminate the problems. Unless you are born into a world where food, shelter and safety are an issue then you are problem free by choice of your own, any problems you do have are a result of the life you lead, the targets you have and the choices you have made."
Acmed smiled and commented,
"Do you think he will give it all up?"
"No he won't but I will tell you this: he is on the brink of collapse, he is about to throw in the towel, he is not going to relinquish all of his power and money but he will take a cut, I could tell that in his voice from the beginning. He is a fool but not that much so."
The man in the office took off his tie completely, he was starting to break, you could see his eyes weaken. As the moments rolled on the assassin and the apprentice watched and listened as the conversation went the way the contract maker had wanted. The stressed man in his office subsided to the demands on him and they ended the phone call. Acmed looked through his scope and watched as the man's shoulders sagged with relief and disappointment at the same time. The assassin took out his earpiece and started to unload his weapon, dismantling it with military ease. The defeated telephone speaker came to his window and opened the frame to the night air. The assassin ready to go whistled and the man looked up; the

assassin blinked a torch at him and shouted across to the building,
"Good choice you now have no more problems."
The man reacted in alarm as he realised what the assassin was talking about and who he was. He looked around into the night sky and spoke back,
"It's a lovely night, a good moon for your work."
The assassin replied,
"You should look at it more often."

VII
THE SUPERMARKET

The blood spread itself over the plastic, driblets of maroon sliding across a transparent sheet, a life come to an end and wrapped in a processed shroud.
"Are you going to buy that steak?" spoke the assassin as Acmed stared through the meat product in his hands, trying to find a vision in his subconscious.
"Sorry I was miles away." The voice of the apprentice was weak and thoughtful. He continued with a speech with an edge of reverb to his monologue.
"Look at those fish, their glaring eyes looking through plastic coffins, we live in a world of murder; the fish murder the plankton and small bait, bigger fish eat those, we eat the fish, the cows and the sheep, the sheep and cows eat vegetation, we truly live in a world of murder. It seems that all must die to produce life, we have surrounded ourselves in the forced impression that we are civilised and are enlightened beings, whilst in reality we are beasts with 'manners', manners that allow us to cannibalise our fellow sentient beings and call it humanity, we live in a strange society."
Acmed looked deep into the plastic coffins and the sterile shelves of the supermarket, his eyes not looking to his master, not here in this take-away temple.
"Come, sit over in the coffee corner young one, lets talk, you look like you are down today, the job is not getting to you is it?"

"No it's not that, in fact it's the opposite. Having watched you kill those people and having killed some myself I am beginning to see humanity with eyes of truth, a true vision that is making me miserable, miserable for their sorry state of affairs."

The two sat in a set of modern fashionable chairs, their acquirement probably an idea by a young pup out of university, trying to make the sanitary ambience of the supermarket appear less obvious. The assassin ordered two hot chocolates, one for him and one for his melancholy friend.

"Master, I don't know what your thoughts are, but I don't see where the human race is going, where are we heading? It seems to me that we are de-evolving our minds and turning into a set of bumbling creatures that have forgotten our roots and stopped any cognitive process, society has become a nation of individuals searching in the dark for more materialistic possessions."

The assassin looked to the waitress as the hot chocolates arrived, steaming jugs of whipped cream mountains with chocolate-flaked slopes.

"Thank you." The assassins' cold eyes could not be masked by his polite gentleman mannerisms and the young girl was set back with caution as she pushed out her reply, backing off.

"You're welcome." and she left with a backward glance.

The assassin tasted those chocolate flakes and sat in a second's joy before he spoke to the apprentice, whose eyes were fixed on the floor.

"Society has taken two major steps in evolution since Neolithic times. I'm not talking of the arrival of democracy, monarchy, oligarchy or any of those attempts at controlling leadership. I'm talking of the industrial revolution and then the evolution of the modern era. Before the industrial revolution life was much simpler. I don't mean to imply that the people were simple or uneducated, in fact it is my firm belief that people were more switched on as humans. Life had a different quality, you had to be more on edge but the clock of life ticked slower and the hours stretched out before you like a wilderness of time. Society revolved more around nature and mother earth; the people were in tune with the community around them and the world in which they lived. Then came the devastation that was the industrial revolution. The rise of the machines, with this we severed the umbilical cord to the womb of the globe. That was the first step we took in de-humanisation, the processed item, thousands of man made objects that were uniform and without originality. It was a grave step for society, the artisan and tradesmen were made redundant and communication stopped between customer and creator. With that link closed, it came to the producer creating the image for the product and there was no input from the buyer. As a result of this the people no longer dictated to the business sector the fashions of the age, they could no longer sway the market in the direction they wished it to advance. This was devastating for society, now they were at the will of the manufacturer. It is they who now controlled the needs of the people which led to the cutting of corners and the loss in standards, for their products were the only ones available and for the cheapest price. Interaction was cut off at the knees, the dealings became one sided."

The assassin put down his cooling cup on to the saucer and crossed his legs, his crisp suit sliding against the chair as he viewed the supermarket in front of him. The apprentice was stirring the melting cream into his mug and his eyes gave a sideward glance for the first time, silently asking the assassin to continue. The assassin placed his cup on the side and continued.

"The second great misfortune came with the modern era, the modern lifestyle which we as humans believe to be the only way we have ever lived and we seem to think it the norm."

The assassin gave an ironic critical smirk as he thought inwardly.

"When I was a boy my grandmother, Mary O'Keefe, the Irish lady she was, used to take me on a Saturday to the shops. First we would hit the chemist, stand in line and say hello to the white-coated gentlemen behind the counter of intoxicating smells and ladies trying on lipstick and makeup. There we would chat to the people around gaining important information on local events and gossip. Then, loaded up with a week's supply of cosmetics, we would go to the newsagents, then to the grocers and then to the butchers. Each time we would talk to the very familiar shop-keepers, giving the news from the last shop and meeting people we knew in the community. For as creatures of habit we tended to go at regular times, meeting a similar pantheon of people each week, forming an inner circle in what was fast becoming a community of individuals. We would do this ritual outing every Saturday. Then on the Sunday we would go to church, again those people would be there, each of the conglomerates that were loose circles of 'shopping-comrades' would interact and spread the gossip and happenings, news, events and troubles of the community. At the time I used to curse them for being doddering old bitches with nothing better to do then talk about the lives of others. Now in the wisdom I have created, I have seen that this was the human race's last ditched effort to keep social communication alive before it died, and trust me my young apprentice, it has died and do you know what was the final nail in the coffin in the death of community life, of knowing your neighbour and their dealings?"

The apprentice took the plastic spoon out of his cup as an incline to continue and the assassin spoke on,

"Well, the death of the village lifestyle was the wretched supermarket, the simple amalgamation of shops into one central empire of commerce. In the town where I shopped with my grandmother, there opened a supermarket. Then as sure as poppies bloom on the fields of battle came the death of each of those shops, the chemist, the butcher, the sweet shop and newsagents all of them one by one boarded up and closed, only to reopen as late night pizzerias and kebab houses and replaced by what? A damn supermarket. Now when we come shopping, instead of huddling into each other's personal space and seeing familiar faces we were struck with the barren emptiness of the whitewashed hall with its air conditioning and false ceiling, where were those familiar ancient faces of my grandmother's friends? We searched aimlessly from aisle to aisle, each long and stocked perfectly, no tit bits to rummage through, just pristine tins in lines. I could see my grandmother wanted to interact with the people trying to drive the new fangled shopping trolley. But why would you stop and talk, there was no need for introduction, strange faces in a strange land. Then as my grandmother aged and died the supermarket was the done thing and the old women of the shops had all passed on. Now no-one talks, they simply push through, rushing around their weekly ritualistic circuit alone and in silence, irritated with queues and people, waiting to arrive at the till where a different women served you each week, no friendly face to recount the tales of the town, just another bored students' visage wishing to be out with their friends. Then recently the last straw has arrived on the camel's back of social extinction, the self-service till. Now a human can go around the desolate hypermarket and arrive at the end to be greeted by a laser scanner and a slot for a credit card, the only familiar thing is the electronic voice issuing a price and receipt. There you have it, the death of society buried under the gravestone of the supermarket, the killer of social interaction."

VIII
DEATH

"Death is for the living."
The assassin stood with his apprentice in the shadow of an oak tree within the graveyard. The mourners passed in polite silence hiding escaping tears, as the pallbearers took the strain of the ebony coffin from the rear of the carriage. Top hats and tails with black plumage and 18-hand steeds. The assassin repeated his words with leafy shadows on his face.
"Death is for the living."
The apprentice in mourning attire reflected the assassin's stance as he whispered,
"You mean that the celebration of death or reflection upon the passing of a loved one is for the comfort of the living left here on earth?"
The assassin uttered without head movement,
"Yes, that's right; those are the basic lines of my thought."
Acmed grimaced through clenched teeth,
"Don't you think its slightly bad manners and inappropriate that we should be attending our own target's funeral, we did kill the man and quite brutally I might add."
The assassin looked to his charge for the first time, that silent few seconds that told him that he was in the wrong, which made the apprentice follow up hastily with,
"I mean, is it not disrespectful to the dead for us to be here?"
The assassin allowed a low toned answer from his firm set jaw,

"It is most proper for us to be here, we may have been the hand of doom that brought about his demise but that was only the demise of the flesh; now we must pay reverence to the soul and the purity of his spirit."

They both began the slow march, lingering at the back of the crowd. The caravan of the corpse made its way to the graveside.

"You see young one, in this day and age we have alienated the Grim Reaper, we have made the Angel of Death stand at a scythe's length, just in reach to kill but not close enough to become a friend and you must make a friend of death, make horror an ally and moral terror a companion in life. If you do not come to terms with this then you will lead a life of fear, a life forever in ignorance of life, for not to embrace death is to live a half life."

The train of people made its way slowly past arched trees and tombs to the dead. The assassin spoke as quietly as possible.

"We were once a nation of strong men and marvellous women, death was there, present since the dawn of time. We would wash the bodies of our fathers, cover their battle wounds and dig holes for them, resting places of the ancestors, communally interred for our remembrance of our line of descent. Now it is a different matter indeed, how many dead bodies has the average person seen, one or two, a grandfather or a great aunt? Then that is when they were prepped and ready for you, changed from their death appearance. A person dies now and we lock the doors so children cannot see them, we wait on the opposite side of the wall as the blackened car of the undertaker makes its way to the house, then we usher them in and wait as we hear them fumbling to put our loved ones in a plastic bag, then like phantom wraiths they are gone and we spend a half of an hour in a room with plastic flowers at some chapel of rest. Making our final visit at the graveside or watching the coffin move through curtains to enter combustion away from our eyes. It's a load of crap; we have detached ourselves from the spirit of our own existence. Mark my words Acmed, the day will come where the people of the west will die, one relative will find them and they will call a government number, then people in white coats will rush to the house and dispose of the body, burning it as contamination and you will receive a nice certificate and plaque and life shall go on without ceremony."

The train of mourners began to make their way from the path, across some grass, to the edge of the grave, filtering slowly.

"You see Acmed, with the modern era comes the age of science and the fall from religion. People mostly don't believe in gods and afterlives now, they believe that this is our one life and there is no more, so care for the spiritual wellbeing of the soul is not imperative. A funeral has changed from preparation rites to aid the soul of the dead to the after life, to a high pomp ceremony that allows the people to mourn and celebrate life to now, an empty modern understanding that is a hollow ritual that people must attend, who are then left with emptiness and grief as they see that the spark of their loved one has gone never to return."

The pair of them stood under the shadow of a Birch tree as the priest dressed in robes of office began to speak and attendees at the rear began to check their watches.

"Can you imagine Acmed the power of a firm belief that they were not dead but transmuted into another form? Imagine how powerful it would be to live in a nation where death was positive and not the end, where you truly believed that you would be reunited. Take the slave girl of the Viking accounts by *Ibn Fadlan*, the slave girl that volunteered to be executed and join her lord on the burning funeral ship. By doing this she became the wife of the lord in the next world, can you imagine, slave to Dame in one cut and she truly believed that she would wake on the other side at her lords' side, so much so to have volunteered death. Take the Egyptian book of the dead, the guide to the other life; the chambered tombs of the prehistoric world that contained the bodies of the ancestors, stripped down to their individual bones and rearranged; public cremation by the Hindu faith on the Ganges River, a journey that will take away their sin; the Japanese funeral rite of passing the uncrushed but cremated bones of the dead between each other using chopsticks. All of these rituals bring you closer to the dead and show a belief in the afterlife. We in our scientific world are closing in fast on the most sterile section of existence that the world has ever known. Do you think that we mere mortals have any concept of the universe around us? We know the meagre fraction of our position in the universe. For as long as man has been aware he has thought of an afterlife and the gods. For our entire existence our ancestors believed in something, it does not matter in what they believed but it is the fact that they had faith, a faith that kept them strong. Our lack of belief is making us weak. It is only now in the last few seconds of human existence that we believe purely in science and science does nothing to answer the spiritual questions; it only can see the physical. What if God exists in some way? What if there is an after life? What if all these millennia our noble ancestors were correct? Then, then our generation is fucked."

The priest was sprinkling some water on the coffin and reciting the words with clinical accuracy.

"That priest, Acmed, is dry and he is an unbeliever. I don't care what he accepts as true, as long as it's something. Think Acmed, if there is an afterlife then using your life to prepare for it and trying to live by an ethical code with the belief in a deity watching over you would be beneficial, because you would be 'rewarded' and accepted in the next world. If it was the case that the afterlife and God did not exist, what harm would it be to live your life in belief, you would be happy to die, happy to pass on, you would live your life by a moral code and you would know nothing of your miss-belief when you did die. There would be no disappointment because you would not exist. I think that is better then living a life of confusion and fear of emptiness. To live a life without purpose would be the greatest fear for me. I will say to you now my young one that I do believe in a god irrelevant of form, religion or name, I simply believe."

Acmed held his face as he was waiting for more and then he spoke,
"So if the identification of the God is irrelevant what gods do you follow?"
The assassin looked to the mourners as they left the graveside and the priest chatted to individuals, then he looked to his young apprentice and said,
"If I follow any incarnation of god it would be Odin and Mars."
The two of them gave a small chuckle and their white teeth illuminated in the shadow of the old Birch tree. Acmed looked to the assassin and spoke,
"He did die a good death did he not? A true warrior's end."
The assassin smiled with pride,
"You did well; yes he died like a true noble man."

IX
GANG MENTALITY

"Packs of rabid dogs, that's what groups of humans are at times, just packs of rabid dogs."

The assassin looked to his apprentice, hinting for an extension on Acmed's words from the blue.

"May I speak my mind, Master?"

"Of course Acmed, you may. I may be master here but we are equal in the world of humanity and all equal in the eyes of the gods, speak to me, never be ashamed to talk your mind."

Acmed sat back against the bench, his eyes looking over the park, over to the dogs playing with their owners, to the dogs that took his mind in this direction.

"Humans are strange, we surround ourselves in pomp and ceremony, pomp that displays to the world that we are civilised, but on the same hand we are monsters and wolves, we are the ultimate in pack hunting, whether its in business or within the confines of modern life or in the more violent arena of the riot. I was watching a documentary the other day on riots. The programme visited scenes from the chaotic football matches of the 1980s to the lootings after natural disasters to the breakdown of African society. I watched in amazement, I have seen masters in Japan, the paintings of Rome, the beauty of sailing magnificent crafts across the sea, but while humans can achieve so much we are only a short step from chaos at any one time."

The assassin slid his remark between his apprentices speech,

"And do you know how far away from chaos we truly are, Acmed?"

Acmed replied his instant voicing,

"I do. We are only ever 3 meals or 24 hours away from chaos, this I do know. Do you remember when all the petrol stations were blockaded at the turn of the century? That was the real eye opener for me. We expect to see riots in third world countries and people stealing from each other en masse but that time when fuel ran out in England, I remember thinking, this is it, we are close. When the fuel ran dry people emergency shopped, they got what they could, then the cars left the road, then the shops were empty, food was gone. I remember going to my friend's house and people had been underneath his car and cut the fuel line to drain the petrol. It was at this point that I knew we were close to anarchy; it was ok when people still had fuel and the shops had bread but after a few days they ran out. I saw it in the faces of the people, they were about to turn, I believe if the army had have not intervened then we would have gone into social meltdown."

The assassin spoke lightly in response to his student as the dogs played in the park,

"Yes, you are right. Civilisation only exists when there is an abundance of food, it is in this civilisation that we gather rules and proper conduct, but nearly all humans will obey this conduct when food is available; it takes a real human to obey those rules when death is doing the *dance macabre*. True, true society is only ever 3 meals away from anarchy or about 24 hours. Once there is no food for that period people start to panic, panic is the mind killer and once the rationality of society has left you revert to the natural state of pack behaviour, the strongest prey on the weak, food and supplies are competition prizes, chivalry and ethics go out of the window. Value is placed on an item depending on its need and availability."

Acmed frowned as he spoke,

"With all due respect, Master, is this my rant or yours?"

The assassin smiled heartily and apologised,

"Forgive me young one, I often take the role of teacher too much sometimes. Please continue with your analysis of society and the state of pack mentality."

They both smiled together and watched as a young woman walking her dog passed them. As she passed Acmed noticed that the assassin had not looked at her once. Strange, why?

"Master why did that women not take your notice, she was very beautiful?"

The assassin came back with a wry face,

"What you are talking about here is the pack mentality showing itself through civilisation, even though society has rules we all still look at pretty women, we fawn over them and dance the cock dance, pleading for their attention, to be truly free of your animalistic state you must be free of ambitions to please the other sex, be calm stay back, wait until you are approached. My master was killed because his flaw was women, control your urges and stay civilised, it is a true civilised human who can hold it together even when faced with the strongest of impulses, now please continue."

Acmed did so,
"I have realised that if you want to push yourself to the limits of human control and if you truly want to be a gentleman in the real sense you must have absolute control over your needs, urges, emotions and instinct. You must retain civility even in the most extreme of circumstances. You must reign in your needs. It is true that humans are animals, but we have risen above the animals of the world, we became king of the jungle over the lion. We hit a pinnacle, the problem is now that we are dropping, lower and lower. With the knowledge that we have acquired we have reached such a height and learnt so much from our forefathers that now we sink below the animals. Humanity started life as an animal – we shared their instincts but we have learnt since then. Like the atom bomb we can't unlearn the technology, we cannot unlearn ethics. So it's with this, when I see a human giving into their needs and urges and killing other humans in a gang mentality, for that I cry for the world. To lower yourself to such a base level is primitively and absolutely evil, an animal will tear you apart because you are food, and humans kill other humans because they support a different football team or because they want something the other has, it is diabolical."
The assassin spoke with an intrigued face,
"You truly feel strong about this don't you?"
"I do master, this hurts me the most. We kill and it's our job, I feel we will pay for it in the afterlife, however, we kill those who cross societies borderlines, you never take a contract that you are uneasy with, you never kill the innocent so if there is

a God I feel he will judge us well. But I have heard that people will kill for a pair of shoes, in some places they kill for fun, gangs of men rape and torture. These people will go to hell if there is one. It is the height of self defeat, they think that they're powerful, they think that they are strong, but they only prey on the weak, it is the divinity of man that he can choose to sacrifice himself for others, that he can hold his urges in times of need. When natural disasters have hit regions you usually hear of the looting, the theft and the murder after, this is because people are scared of death, they fear the unknown realm of life without society. It is so refreshing to see people help others in times of need, it is a boost to my confidence when those in danger pull together and help others."

The assassin watched as two dogs began to sniff at each other,

"Well young one, I can see that I am rubbing off on you, you are starting to think, you are starting to become alive. If I could teach you anything it would be this: learn to control yourself, not when all around is ok, but when you most need control, in panic. When you feel panic rise you must do a self-analyses, panic profits man nothing, and panic kills civility. Emotion is good in small doses, to give into emotion is to fall beneath the animal kingdom, and once you have been a king you never want to be a slave, but a slave only knows the life of a slave and dreams of being a king. If you are the king turned slave then you have hatred and resentment in you, if you are a slave dreaming you have hope. Hope is the genesis for chivalry and the driving force of manners and ambition. Therefore, like you say Acmed, a man who

drops his ethics in a time of crisis is indeed a man on the decent to hell, and if this man is followed by several more than several hundred you have gang mentality. Also, what you did not raise was the point that man as an individual is responsible for his actions, in a group he is masked by uniformity, he is in line with the group ethics, he is one cog in the wheel of destruction. You see by himself he is scared of the consequences of his actions, as a pack they are free to do as they please as the courts of today cannot prove without doubt that he was involved, so, there is the vent for his animalistic nature, there is his get-out clause...so if you could say anything now apprentice what would it be?"
Acmed spoke with thought,
"I would say that if you wanted to be a better human and a true gentleman or lady, then you must be self-analytical, you must take control of your urges and push yourself to the limits, you must be ready to die before letting go of your ethics, defend yourself in times of need but share your bounty and drive for normality when all around is chaos."
As Acmed stopped the two dogs snarled and began to fight, they lashed at each other as their owners pulled them apart.

X
LITTER

A nonchalant man tossed his empty cigarette packet onto the floor.
The assassin walked over to him, drew out a gun and shot him point blank, through the teeth, a fountain of dentistry.

XI
MODERN SOCIETY & THE MEANING OF FREEDOM

The traffic light was on red, a striking warning ablaze in the foggy streets of London; Big Ben loomed in the lunar glow against a nocturnal sky. The assassin sat in the passenger seat as Acmed the apprentice manned the wheel. The sapphire silence was broken by the assassin's amber-honey voice coming from the shadows.

"If society collapsed tomorrow we would still drive on the left hand side of the road."

Acmed looked in his mirrors to check around him and spoke as he observed,

"Surely if society collapsed the cars would not run and society would revert to a pre-industrial state of agriculture and sedentary farming."

"Of course it would Acmed, but in the few years post to its demise the relics of the modern age would hold on for dear life, fuel would be worth more then human life and mechanics would be the high priests of the day, equivalent to the smith kings of Iron Age Europe. Anyway my statement was meant to be conversationally provocative in nature."

Acmed looked over to the master assassin as he put the car in first gear and pulled away as the amber lights switched to a vibrant green.

"Ohh."

The assassin continued as they drove past the statue of Queen Boadicia,

"You see modern society is a Neuro-Linguistic-Programming system on a massive scale, ninety percent of the world are trained from birth to react within a given framework by their governments and are not to stray outside those boundaries, boundaries that are contrary to human emotion and instinct."

Acmed interjected as he rounded a foggy corner, illuminated in tawny street lamps,

"Ah, but I must protest, surely civilisation is based on the fact that we can overcome our animal instincts, we can rise above natural urges, transcend the needs of purely functional activities such as consumption, fornication, shelter-building and defence. Is it not the ability to establish surplus nutrition to aid a freedom of time-management that allows us to promote the non-practical, the arts, theatre, poetry, history, art, the sciences and all the other interpretive states that the mind can achieve in all their related genres? The structure of modern society is based on this theory. Surely that is not a bad thing?"

The assassin looked at his young apprentice for a few seconds provoking a prompt from the questioning youth.

"What… what is that face for?"

The assassin smiled and looked out of the window, out in to the mist of the midnight air as he spoke to the world outside as well as his young passenger,

"I did not know that you were passionate for the world we live in?"

Acmed replied with a slight withdrawal,

"Well maybe I am slightly proud of the human machine; I can see the heights that the human civilisation can achieve."

Then he continued with a thought and a lower tone,

"Also its gross base, man's inhumanity to man."

The assassin waited to see if Acmed had more to say but upon his apprentice's silence he continued his lesson.

"If society failed, then I would bet you my life that if a lone driver was driving at night and a red light switched itself on then he would screech to a halt and he would find himself on the correct side of the road. This is just my example to say that as 'civilised' true society yielded to the modern era we allowed ourselves to be shaped and programmed by the world around us. This world made us fit into its shape, a shape that did not form so well around the human ethos. Society today has trapped itself in its own bureaucracy and rules, become a prisoner of its own laws. Simple things like you cannot carry a weapon. To the modern reader it seems alien to even think of a society where people walk the streets armed. Tell that to the early modern humans or the Neanderthal that he is not allowed his spear or knife, he is allowed nothing to protect himself with. Take away the sword of a knight, the axe of a Viking and tell them that they cannot hold a weapon for defence. Don't think for an instant that life is any different now then it was then in terms of threat. There are still people out there, people who wish to kill and maim you for no other reason then self-satisfaction but here and now the police say no to protection, they say they will deal out the law. Do the criminals stop themselves carrying weapons? No. They continue to arm themselves and kill and maim. The only difference is now, that law-abiding citizens no longer carry arms and what used to be a hard task or a threat to the criminal is now easy prey and a vulnerable subject. I know that if I lived in a society where every one carried a knife and was trained, and allowed to engage in combat then I would think twice about approaching that person. That method is a dead relic of an ancient way, how we have trapped ourselves into believing that a stab in the dark and group mugging are a state of affairs we must accept and deal with, calling it an unlucky event. Luck has nothing to do with it, the rule of eye for an eye is gone, and the new rule is they take your eye and you cry about it and that's it. Even if you wished to take vengeance upon your enemy, society has taken that right away from you. If my children were raped and murdered, my wife violated and hacked to pieces I would be arrested for exacting vengeance. The people in the street would say I had cause, each individual law officer would sympathise and condone what I had done but as a nation they would have to prosecute me. No one would agree that I should go to prison after such a heinous crime against me but I would have to go because we are all programmed to believe that the system must be upheld. Systems are only upheld because of universal belief in that said system, a belief that is forced subconsciously upon us but unanimously repelled against at the human base level. Even grandmothers, sweet and old would have a paedophile hanged by the testicles and cut from ear to ear. There is a natural law that we hold as humans but it is forced out by society's dogmatic attempts to quell the human spirit.

The apprentice looked over to the stern face of the assassin as he ploughed through the mist and rain.

"And what of guns? By armed do you mean guns? For if you are saying that it should be eye for an eye and tooth for tooth, then if they have a knife, then we have a knife? But what if they get a gun, what then? We get bigger ones running into chaos?"

The assassin put his finger in the air and spoke with authority.

"Never, the gun is not a weapon but a mistake of man, I use a gun but that is simply because to not do so would be to invite an untimely death, in this business anyway."

He gave a strange smile as he moved on,

"The gravest thing man ever did was invent the gun, until that point men were not equal, men were born, inherited and cultivated strengths. The gun took that natural selection away and allowed the wicked, weak and easily malleable to take control. Of course people were wicked in a pre-firearms society but back then if you pushed it too far you would find your head on the top of a pole. Now the true horror of the gun has made even the lions of men mice, lions against vermin with automatic weapons. If the gun was not invented then today would be a different story, truly different."

Acmed looked to him and questioned,

"How so?"

"Well we always look at the past as a collection of tribes, clans or gangs, the hardest and strongest were the leaders. The most powerful were at first the leaders and tacticians, defenders of the family groups, then as time went on the powerbase of each grew in size until a country was filled and boundaries could go no further. Then came the enlightenment, democracy and the new era where this tribal war was no more. Well this is an untruth. Even the Kings and Queens of England and other great nations were at the mercy of the other powerful clans. It is commonly believed that the monarch held sway over all, in reality the monarch was only in power as they had the most support from a coalition of the other dukes, barons and aristocracy. It was a delicate peace between massive power houses and the monarch only held sway by a slight amount, this can be seen in the fact that monarchs were commonly overthrown and new dynasties were established but all this was done with the sword. Then, enter the modern GUN! This was it, the age of stable power ended. Now the aristocracy could not force the monarch out of their seat, soon the monarch called for a unified army, under their banner alone. Then other aristocrats could not hold personal armies, then the populace could not own a gun and then in the end we are not allowed to carry knives or swords. Some monarchies turned into Prime Ministers and Presidents but they are all the same. If you think that with the modern era we have left clan and gang warfare in the past you are a fool. How big a gang is the army, the police and the government? They are the biggest gangs the world has ever seen but we think that it is a forward thinking society, they demand money from us, tell us not to carry protection and because they install their demands in the appearance of forms and printed material with code numbers and mechanical uniformity we think it is ok, we are programmed to think that if it has an official stamp on it then it's a progressive utility. Tell me Acmed, what is the definition of a protection racket, what is the definition of extortion?"

Acmed pulled up at a set of traffic lights as they turned red and smiled to himself.

"The definition is a stronger force, taking a percentage of your income, with the intention to defend you against other gangs or external hostile forces."

Acmed shrugged his shoulders towards the assassin and the assassin replied with academic eagerness,

"And now what is the definition of income tax?"

Acmed smiled in understanding.

The definition is a stronger force, taking a percentage of your income, with the intention to defend you against other gangs or external hostile forces."

The assassin spoke with a hell blaze in his eyes,

"Exactly, and which army of peasants armed with pitchforks will take on her majesty's armed forces?"

Acmed let out a laugh and the assassin continued,

"Humans are entitled to a certain amount of freedom and that freedom is:"

Human Freedom
Entitlements

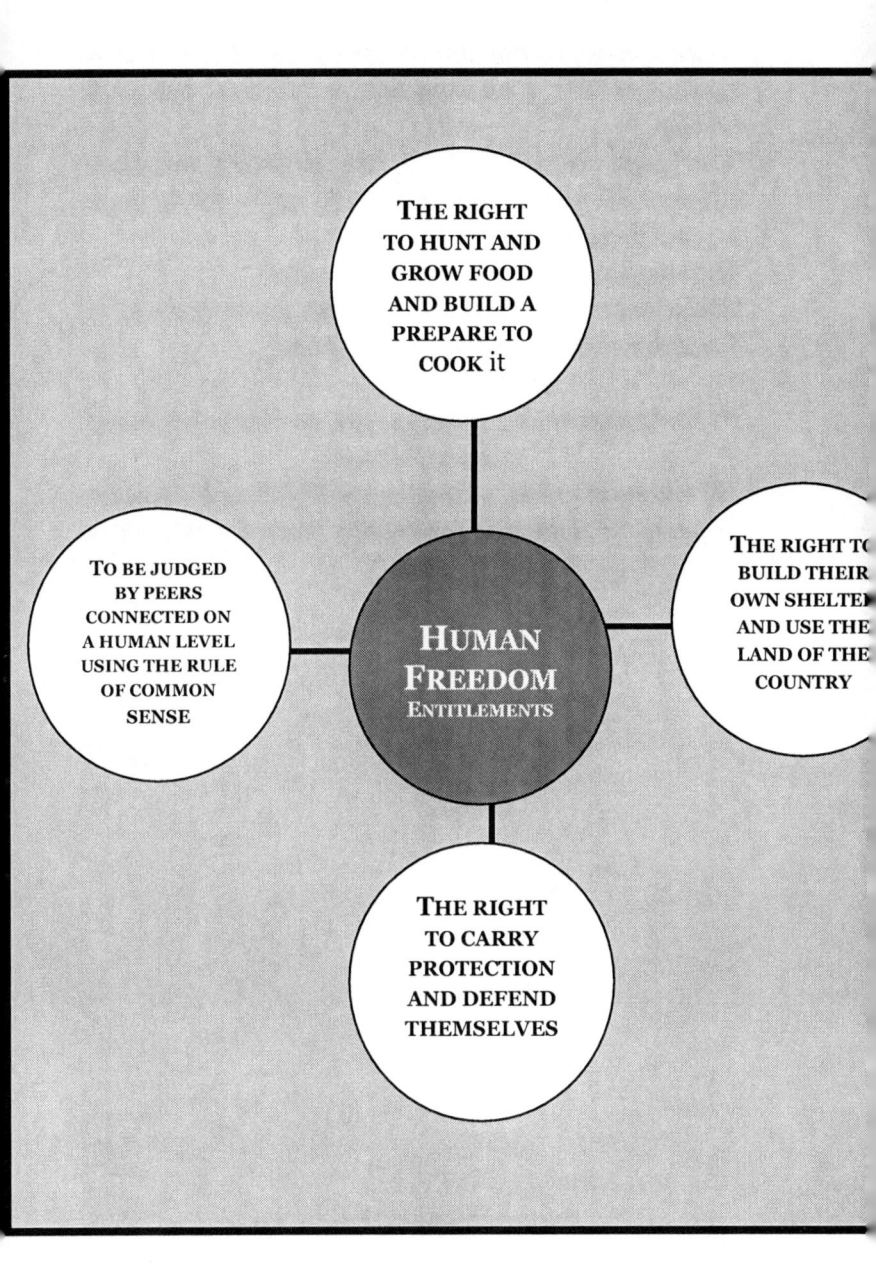

- **The right to hunt and grow food and build a prepare to cook** it
- **The right to build their own shelter and use the land of the country**
- **The right to carry protection and defend themselves**
- **To be judged by peers connected on a human level using the rule of common sense**

Acmed agreed with the assassin and confirmed his agreement with a nod but held a quizzical eye as he asked,
"But even though your theory is sound the sheer volume of people on the earth calls for a more sophisticated system of control."
The assassin smiled with a hidden glee,
"Quite correct my young apprentice, quite correct."
The assassin looked directly at Acmed,

"While there are too many men on this earth there must be laws,
While laws exists, corruption will fill men's hearts
There will always be laws while there are too many men."

XII
RELIGION

The Vatican City was illuminated in crimson sunlight as the fire-chariot set on another day of the world of humanity, as it has set for the earth countless times across many empires. The lone assassin and cub sat at the entrance to the avenue and square that led up to Saint Peter's. They watched as passers-by came and went, hopeful tourists, pilgrims and the generally interested. Each one of them passed the ancient women kneeling by the roadside, her rosary held high, drowning in the sunset rays and the ignorance of the world around her but yet she stayed unanimated, no pleas for coin, no cry on the mercy of the public, just a simple kneeling human, arms held up in prayer and cap on the floor with limited donations as guilt-reminding as her upturned Christ-like eyes.

"What do you think she is doing young one?"

The assassin did not look to his apprentice as they sat at a table outside a café observing the general populace, sunset making their eyes narrow with sharpness.

"It is clear as day, she is praying."

"Is it now, and tell me who is she praying to?"

The apprentice turned with suspicion, the question was too obvious to have hidden answers. He tried to search the assassin's face for a tell-tale sign that would show which way the answer lay, but as always the face was a perfect emotionless blanket of confusion.

"I would say it was that clear yes, she is an obviously catholic women of Italian birth holding a rosary, with an image of the Virgin Mary and she is kneeling outside the Vatican City. I would say she is praying to the Christian God."

The assassin picked up his coffee cup and spoke before he took a sip,

"No, she is not praying to God, she is appealing to the ingrained ethics that religion promotes."

Acmed squinted in puzzlement as the assassin sipped from the white cup, froth stained,

"I understand your basic direction but why would she not be praying to God?"

The assassin placed the porcelain cup back on the saucer,

"Do you think that, deep down, that woman who has lived here all her life, adopted that pose day in and day out, praying to God, has not had her doubts as to why he has not showered her in gold for the religious dedication she has shown? Furthermore, if she was a true believer and happy to spend her days in silence on her knees, why has she not moved to a mountain? She parades her fake hermit persona in public and if that was her true vocation she would have gone into mountain seclusion where food is abundant and solitude the currency of life, no she is not praying to God."

The apprentice questioned as he drank from an identical cup,

"Ok then, what do you mean by ingrained ethics of religion?"

The assassin sat back as he began his monologue,

"Religion, often wrongly blamed for the conflict in the world, was created for what reason, to praise an omnipotent being?"

He opened his palms as the question echoed.

"No, it was not. Before I divulge this lesson I want to get one thing clear."
The assassin lent forward to aid strength to his words,

"GOD IS GOD, RELIGION IS MAN MADE."

He sat back and continued,
"No, religion is not about gods, it's about a code of ethics, a set of rules to live life by. Ancient people understood that humans had an ingrained basic law system, a system of basic right and wrongs that allowed us to live in harmony with each other and the world around us. It is a set of laws that are common to all religions, do not kill, steal, injure or defile others. Keep the world and beasts around you in harmony and do not push Mother Nature out of line, rest when needed and give charity to support the needy. These laws were not written down, they were basic common sense understood by most people, and it was only a few bad apples in a bunch that crossed this line. Did you know the archaeological evidence for warfare in the Neolithic is a fraction of the amount you get when we turned to the Iron Age, an era that boosted agricultural tools and productivity, leading to a population explosion, before this it was possibly close to the true Eden. Before the need to codify the ethical rules they were held as common law among mankind but as this population explosion erupted on the surface of the globe the requirement arose to justify them and outline the rules of engagement for a, now highly integrating,

humankind. I truly believe these first religious doctrines were pure and true, giving the true teachings of how to live your life. However, as the corruption of the dogmatisation rule creeps into men's hearts so does the selection and interpretation of these texts. Extracts are highlighted and abused, elements chosen over others and the context misplaced. Take the Jewish food laws. Separation of cutlery that deal with dairy and meat products must be strictly separated. In biblical times, in the heat of the near east this is common sense, but in a modern kitchen with hygiene and refrigeration the rule is left misplaced and unneeded. Now, take Muslim burial rites, in some divisions of the faith the body must be in the ground within the day. That's all well and good in arid heat where disease and infection via contamination is life threatening. No, it is dogmatisation and the inability to take the positive elements from something pure into the next generation that are the downfall of organised religion. They try to fit into codes that no longer have meaning and all because it has been written down, once written forever quotable, once quotable forever dogmatised. If Christians, Muslims, Jews and all the other religions of the world truly followed their own code, if they open-heartedly and honestly opened up to the codes and laws that they followed then there would be no religion, just the congregation of the 'children of humanity'. If this was the case you would never hear terms such as: The 'infidel', 'thou shall not endure a witch to live', 'death to the unbeliever', 'Crusade', 'Jihad' and all the other religious corruptions. If Muslims, Christians and Jews truly looked into their hearts they would see that they are all one and that they fight not over religion but over supremacy and egotism, a fight that has no end."

Acmed looked behind him to see what had taken the assassin's attention from him. It was a cardinal, dressed in the scarlet robes of his office, laced in gold trim and precious stones. The assassin spoke with venom.

"Here comes the product of hierarchical obsession, if he truly believed in the word of God to the level his office requires he would be dressed as plain as snow and have a mind that pure."

Acmed nodded silently and the assassin continued,

"The church, no matter what denomination, started humble, with truly spiritual men taking hold of the flock they served, leading them to true salvation and understanding. Even though men have wickedness inside them, the few true would attempt to lead them properly. But with this spirituality came position and veneration, veneration that was deserved but it was also converted by less pious men, not evil but less pious. These lesser men emulated the deeds of the higher orders and took undeserving positions, then as time and generations endure the positions become structured and revered, coming with examination and requirements. However, these positions still held the power and veneration of the public as it was ingrained in their psyche over time. So, naturally, as these positions were held in high office they were converted by power hungry souls whose goal was not the harmony of the people or the want for ethical codification and adherence. It was the greed of evil men, who used the pure religious texts to their own

ends, supporting their aggressive self promotions with biblical sanction."
The cardinal was getting closer to the café. He was coming alongside and the conversation between master assassin and apprentice stopped to allow him to pass. As he passed the self-love was evident in his stride. Acmed physically gasped as the noble of the religious world walked past the kneeling women without a glance or acknowledgement. Not a single recognition of a fellow soul in need. Acmed spoke,
"Religion is truly lost and I did not see it until now."
The assassin chirped with humour,
"Then you were blinded by the programming of society, don't take anything on face value, if you start to think about most things you will realise they have no worth and are preposterous."
The assassin stood up and began to move towards the women.
"It's a good job that I follow the true meaning of religion in some ways."
With this he handed her €2000 and spoke in Italian,
"Equality among men."
Then changed his accent to revering and spoke out so that his target could hear him,
"Cardinal, may I have your blessings?"
The cardinal turned and upon seeing the sharply dressed assassin smiled and approached. The assassin kissed the rings on his finger and slipped his right hand into his pocket, gripping what he needed.
"Your grace."

XIII
PHILOSOPHY

"Why are we on our way to kill a professor?"
Acmed quizzed as they walked across the university campus with its gothic architecture and lush green lawns.
"The lovers of knowledge have political views that usually outweigh the rest of the populace, however, this one took too far a step into a political world he should not have ventured into, his writings are becoming too damaging."
Came the assassins reply. Acmed smirked as he asked the next question,
"The lovers of knowledge? I take it you are referring to the etymology of the word 'philosophy', literally 'a love of knowledge'?"
The assassin smiled in his crisp black suit, university cap and gown.
"Very astute young one, that's why I chose you to be my next in line, when I am gone or have retired you will take my place and kill in my stead, then you must pass on this profession to the next and I recommend that you chose someone with a love of knowledge, otherwise you are choosing a dead soul."
The apprentice spoke holding academic journals under his arm.
"Recently I have been thinking of knowledge and what it means to us. I think the 'phil' or the 'love' of knowledge has left the world, or not the world as such, but to the masses, it seems only a few strive for the search of knowledge."

The assassin cleverly investigated with his next sentence,

"So you think people of the past were more astute and intellectual?"

To which the apprentice spoke,

"No, not at all, but I think the world they lived in drove them to search for knowledge and accomplishments, you see today you walk out of your front door and buy the paper, a snack, go shopping for food and buy some clothes and jewellery and then retire to your armchair or computer. What need is there to do anything? In fact it is that exact need to not do anything that has led to the problems of obesity and sloth. Can you make a fire from nothing? Can you speak another language or several dialects of your own? Do you know how to skin and gut an animal? If you do then you are a better being then most. In my opinion everyone from queen to beggar should have the knowledge of how to survive from starting with nothing. If you cannot do this then you have lost basic, and I mean *basic*, human skills. If everyone in the world turned round at the same time and tried to achieve these basic things the television companies would collapse and food shops take a massive loss in profit and the pockets of the individual would fill up."

The two fell silent as they passed a group of students on the floor and Acmed started again when they had passed,

"Putting aside basic human skills and knowledge, there is the development of other knowledge that is good for society. They no longer teach Latin and ancient Greek in schools and why not? It is deemed as unusable and a waste of time, codswallop! You see I believe that [society has become so capitalist and 'modern' that it deems knowledge that can only be used for profit and accomplishment in a fiscal form] We learn business and market ethics but as we are so young when we learn this it transfers to our system of normal ethics and teamwork and social unity are not ingrained within us. Instead [competition and rivalry are instilled in our souls] The ancients had a tougher struggle for life; their knowledge was concentrated on the opposite and the ability to survive as a unity. As there was no need for capital gain, as a disposable income was not needed, they concentrated on more self-fulfilment and constructive pastimes. Anything from simple carving to herb and tree recognition to the complexities of Ancient Greek politics or the hidden subtleties of the Japanese theatre world of Kabuki would exercise the mind."

The assassin did not say a word he just smiled as they walked through the hidden corridors and the maze of offices in this archaic building. They walked past rows and rows of oak doors until they came to the prescribed one, with letters of gold.

SIR EDWARD DOMINICAN-MORT PHD
DOCTOR OF ARCHAEOLOGY & HISTORICAL MARTIAL ARTS ADVISOR TO THE CROWN

The assassins knocked on the door and waited for, "Enter."

The two came in to an ancient and thin man, maybe once of a powerful frame. The room was a cabinet of curiosity, full of relics and old wood, honey and whiskey windows behind him with books from wall to wall. Upon the desk was a *Fetchbück*, a medieval German fighting manual for Knights of Europe, a foreboding addition to the collection. The old knight and philosopher looked to them and then back to his writing pad but with realisation he looked up slowly.
"So, assassin and cub, you have come…finally."
The assassin was slightly taken back.
"How do you know, sir?"
The academic-warrior answered with a smile, putting down his ancient quill,
"You are wearing the new crest for the school, that new motto was only added three years ago, you must be what, forty years old, sir? If you are a true doctor of this establishment you would still be wearing the old crest like you are entitled to. I take it the handsome young man next to you is your apprentice, he seems correct with the new crest due to his age."
"He is, sir?"
The assassin looked respectfully humbled but the Knight broke the silence,
"Sit down, make yourself comfortable."
The two sat down and the assassin regained the slight control he had lost,
"Sir Edward, my apprentice and I were just discussing the use of non-profitable knowledge."
The knight looked up and said,
"I presume you are talking about profit in a fiscal sense."
The assassin nodded and the old doctor continued,

"Of course financially profitable knowledge is the least profitable in a spiritual sense. But my dear man, all knowledge is priceless; knowledge is what brings us above the beasts of the forest. To be human and have cognitive thought."

Acmed addressed the Knight for the first time,

"Sir Knight, I feel that my generation have the ingrained understanding that knowledge for knowledge sake is a miserable loss of time, it's as though we are bred to believe if we are not earning, then anything else is a waste of effort and that we are not amounting to anything."

The Knight sat back and smiled,

"True, true, I feel for your generation, you have been given a bad deal, you have been left wanting. The love of knowledge is the godliest gift we have. Those who show a love for knowledge have a quicker mind and more astute sense of the world, plus they don't feel inclined to violence and destruction. My true dream was to die an old man surrounded by books, full of knowledge and a real loss to the world, a keeper of knowledge."

The Knight paused and looked with a smile,

"I suppose that is how I am going to die…is it not, Master assassin"?

The assassin gave a respectful bow and nodded,

"You will die a true gentleman."

Acmed broke the silence,

"But is it not a waste to gather all that information and then die, losing it all, what is the point?"

The ancient knight smiled, kind and warm,

"I thought that once, what a waste to learn so much and then to die, losing it all. But you should realise that life is not about the end goal but about the journey, the richness of life that you lead, if you have died with all that knowledge then you die a king among men. As well as this, young one – I firmly believe, no, I *know*, that you will go on to an afterlife and we may not take that specific knowledge with us but we will take the essence of the experience, if you die a moron and a loaf you will take negativity with you to the next world. If you die rich in mind you will be a golden beam of light, travelling along in silk…remember these words boy, I hope you will live to achieve what I have."

The old Knight stood up and opened a cupboard, the oak wood opened up to reveal a red velvet interior. He took out an antique pole-arm, a spear of old and walked to the centre of the room; he forced the spiked butt into the floor and the spear shook with vibration as it stood erect.

"This is for my head when you have taken it master assassin."

The assassin nodded in silence; next the old knight reached into the weapons rack and pulled out an exquisite bastard sword, clad in dark leather, solid and old. The Knight drew the sword in one and a fire glared in his archaic eyes,

"To die by the sword, a true and noble death."

His words whispered as he looked up and down the pattern-welded blade with love. Then as though he snapped out of a trance he offered the assassin the hilt and spoke,

"Master assassin, if you will give me a true and noble end?"

The Assassin gave a full bow and held the hilt of the sword as the Knight let go. Then he spoke,
"Sir Knight, I am humbled by you, forgive me and please accept my humble hand in your execution."
The knight smiled,
"Accepted."
The Knight pulled from his draw a comb and combed his grey hair back, then reached into a draw for some oil, he put the scented oil on his hair and breathed in the smell. Slowly he moved to the centre of the room and knelt down. Taking a last glance at the *Fetchbück* on the desk, he lowered his eyes and head and spoke.
"I offer you my head master assassin; please take it in the spirit it is offered."
"I do." came the reply and with a single blow the assassin sliced off the head of the kneeling Knight. Blood-drenched and stained was the floor of brandy coloured wood. The assassin picked up the head and stuck it with reverence on the spike. He brushed the hair back into place with his hand and cleaned the sword, replacing it in its sheath and within the cabinet. He looked to his apprentice and said thus,
"I am humbled by such a noble being; true was his nobility, a true human."
With this the assassin bowed his head in honour and the two left the room in silence.

XIV
GREED

The restaurant was expensive, decadent in extreme and full of the wealth and trappings of the affluent. The assassin and the apprentice were dressed sharp and elegant, no expense spared. Drinking from crystal and dining of the best china. The two were eating delicate amounts and engaging in philosophical debate when the waiter interrupted them.
"Sir, may I ask if you are enjoying the meal?"
The assassin placed his fork down and replied,
"Most divine, my compliments."
"That is wonderful sir, may I state that there is a gentleman who wishes to remain anonymous, and he wishes to take over the bill for you and would like me to deliver this envelope."
With that the waiter placed with hidden gestures a stiff envelope on the table next to the assassins hand, its paper crisp, the calligraphic hand black and flowing on its front.
"Thank you, give my regards to my benefactor and wish him well."
"Very good, sir."
The assassin looked to the envelope, slid it slowly up from the table and opened its contents. The apprentice could see his master hold a hand written letter and a photograph.
"What is it?"
The eagerness of the apprentice could be heard slightly in his voice and the assassin replied slowly,
"A job, a new target."

The assassin placed the contents back in the envelope and slipped his new cargo into his inner pocket.

"This restaurant is where I pick up my contacts and kills, you shall use it when I am gone. Simply place a cup inverted on a saucer and people will come to you."

Acmed realised for the first time that the cup in front of his master was inverted. The assassin spoke,

"Now where were we in our debate of the day?"

The apprentice replied,

"We were discussing greed."

"Ah, so we were. Now let me see where were we, ah I remember, the man over in the far corner, the fat grotesque beast eating enough food for troop at the charge of the light brigade. Look at him, pompous and grotesque in his appearance, manner and stature, greed, the vile sin of man."

Acmed spoke with surprise,

"You don't half seem annoyed by that man."

The assassin responded with hidden disgust,

"That creature is probably some fattened up politician, the filth of life. He has money to burn, the leisure time to indulge in anything he wishes, he is the top end of society yet what does he do, give in to greed! Fucking idiot!"

The apprentice was taken aback and the assassin changed his tone as he continued, changed it to be more inline with his surroundings.

"You see Acmed we have lost the fight for survival, humans no longer need to fight for food in any first world country. We simply follow society's rules and gain pretend money and spend it in the supermarket. The problem is this; when you gather and make your own food you expend energy to do so, so the more you eat the more energy you have to expend, giving a natural balance. But now or even in ancient times for those who rose to power and wealth the story is much different. For them the production of food is a case of money spending, a venture that does not use up any energy, a venture that leads to obesity. But obesity is another issue, the issue in hand here is the need to eat and eat, take and take, to give into greed. I believe that when you truly work for something, you have an end goal that you reach through effort and then the 'taste' or experience of the goal is delicious and filling, you appreciate the rewards with the sent of an animal, in waves and waves. If you have true satisfaction in this end result you are content and at ease within yourself, however, if you have not worked for the product then your outlook is different indeed. The 'taste' and experience of something you have not worked for is not as sweet as you would want, and the 'fix' is not quite enough to hold you over. You become indifferent to the experience; it does not hold any magic or have a profound edge to it. Due to this lack of satisfaction you quest for more and more indulgence to fulfil your human psychological needs, simply eating enough does not suffice. As a result of trying to fill these gaps you take on the consequences, that of obesity or the corruption of the soul and the absence of charity from your being."

The apprentice finished chewing and spoke as he picked up his drink,

"So do you class excessive food consumption and the accumulation of material wealth as greed?"

"Yes I do Acmed; indeed, they are one and the same thing, look to the centre left ahead of you, look at that man's suit, his watch and his cuff links, even down to the embroidered napkin, he indulges in material wealth, you can tell that he has numerous amounts of goods stored and unused. This to me is the same as a greed for food. To him the goods he buys are meaningless; he has not worked for them nor tasted poverty. Each time he buys something it is a temporary fix for that moment of boredom. Once that moment has gone he is uninterested in what he has bought, for him it is not owning the product but simply the high of buying expensive items, his thrill is being watched at the counter, being seen with bags from expensive shops and the feeling of wellbeing by accumulation. His life is truly void of understanding; he is a ghost filling his life by touching the human need of fulfilment by a string of short bursts of false achievement. If he spent his time striving to achieve something else, an art or a skill he would find that the need for spending would die down, he would relish his time and appreciate what else he has, forgoing the need to spend."

Acmed countered, over his mouth-watering dessert,

"So you are saying that extravagance and expense are greed? But don't you yourself indulge in the expensive world?"

"Not so Acmed, of course I indulge in expensive luxury items but that is not the argument, everybody buys within their price range, it's not the amount you spend on an item but the amount of items you possess. It's ok to have expensive suits and an expensive car, but I don't need 30 suits and I don't

need three cars, which is the point. It's a reliance on accumulation not the amount you spend that determines your greed. If I was a greedy person and I had the realisation of my faults I would go through every single one of my belongings and categorise them into needed and unneeded. Then I would give all the unneeded ones away to charity. To live a sparten life is the true way of living, to live as a minimalist is the path of perfection. Buy as many books as you like, have as many CDs as you wish. Music and knowledge are the keys to life, or art, anything that provokes a continuous emotion, such as films or poetry is accepted, but anything that is discarded after use to a cupboard is unnecessary. Surround yourself with emotion provoking elements and strive to achieve skills in your life, turn off that TV and learn to paint, write, play anything you wish, as long as what you buy provokes a response you will find that the need to accumulate drops away."
Acmed chirped in,
"You can't take it with you I guess."
"True, true, but when you go you can leave a treasure chest of richness for someone to inherit, not with fiscal worth but educational, something to stir the feelings, to give a message to the right side of the brain, something to be remembered by."
Acmed and the assassin finished their meal and ate the thin delicate slice of chocolate, a smooth aftertaste to the slight but sufficient meal just eaten.
"I love fine food, fine art, fine music and a fulfilling life young Acmed and I tell you this now, none of these feelings are achieved through greed. Greed is the surfacing monster of a weak mind, a mind that

constantly tries to find meaning in life. The meaning in life is to fulfil it."
"Yes, Master."

XV
LOVE

The cinema was dark, musty and old, the dust filled light from the projection reminded the assassin of the old days, when one could smoke during the film. The screening of the day was not a classic or a black and white re-showing, it was a new film, filled with CGI and marvels of technology but still the cinema was old, a relic of a bygone world, crammed with new technology. The assassin and Acmed sat at the back, the dark partially illuminated by the reflections of the images. The target sat four rows down, his head transfixed on the screen, rhythmically placing popcorn into his mouth, interspersed by trips to his straw for sweet liquid refreshment. The assassin paid him no attention, there were few people in the auditorium and all eyes were on the screen. Out of the blue the assassin whispered, almost unheard,
"Are you the type of person who is star struck Acmed?"
Acmed pondered the question,
"There are a few film stars I would like to meet and maybe a few musicians but on the whole no not really."
"Me neither but would you say that the populace are star struck?"
"Oh most definitely, I think most of our time is spent surrounded by the stars, models and musicians. Since modern technology arrived the ability to project the individual into our lives has become commonplace, with the print and the TV we have a catalogue of people we 'know'."

"Very good Acmed, very good, and what do you think of that? Do you think people love their stars, there famous 'visitors' to the home?"

Acmed contemplated and whispered back,

"Yes I think they do, I think that people love their stars, they fawn after them and they worship them as idols in a way. Each generation has a list of people that they are all familiar with, some more then others, and it can become a focal point for people, a shared identity, as like music and bands, people share the experience and the imagery. It creates a type of floating tribe without boundaries."

The assassin responded,

"But is that love?"

Acmed whispered back,

"I believe it is a type of love. A passion shared maybe?"

The assassin sat back in his chair and spoke again,

"Imagine this; there is a premier showing in Hollywood. Johnny Depp is the lead star and he is walking on the red carpet, the lights are flashing, Winona Ryder is in the area, the fans are screaming, the night is loud. Suddenly the barrier breaks and the people surge forward. The border between the common mass and the stars breaks. What happens next?"

Acmed responded slowly and quietly,

"The crowd would rush them and touch them and try to converse with the stars, I think they would be bounced around a bit but I think they would come to no harm. They would simply be the focus of extreme attention."

"The focus of love?" quizzed the assassin and Acmed thought before he spoke.
"I think so."
The lights of the film dimmed down, leaving the cinema in near blackness. An explosion from the previous scene still rumbled with terrifying surround-sound as the light faded. With a quick motion the assassin brought a form of pipe to his lips, a sleek and slender carbon cylinder. With a short blast of air, drowned by the cinematic roar, a dart flew towards the target. With a snap of his hand the target grabbed his neck, but no sooner had his hand reached the projectile menace than it slipped back down again, in unison with the target's head – unconscious – then dead. The assassin began pulling on a thin section of fishing line and Acmed could see the dart bouncing slowly across the arched seats of this ancient arena. As the master assassin pulled the cord and dart home he whispered again,
"Now imagine the same scene again, Mr Depp is there, red carpet and all, but this time the flashes are not born of camera, but are the products of a terrorist attack. Nail-bombs and explosives rip through the air, tearing bodies apart. Crimson life flows over the red carpet and people break the barriers. What do they do this time, do they run to touch the stars, and do they wish to converse with them…no, of course not, for what they have is not love, but false love. In this moment the reality of life and feelings is thrust upon you, it is in these times that your conscious self can no longer weave the fabricated story of your own existence, the grudges and squabbles you held blow away, the raw emotions and proof of who you truly

love comes out at these times. [We live in a world where false love reigns supreme and why? Because we live in a comfortable place, we have an abundance of what we need, we have no real threats in our life, and therefore we cloud our minds to whom we really love. Love, one of the rawest of passions we own and one of the most truthful; we know who is truly important to us in extremities. People should do an analysis of their lives, people should hold in their minds that at any moment life can be torn apart and death can come on his pale horse and change your life instantaneously.] If people held this emotion in their hearts at all times the amount of grudges would drastically shorten. My apprentice you should forget about any stars or celebrities, even those minor ones in your own life, those people you put on a pedestal within the boundaries of your own existence. You should imagine the world torn apart by war, then ask yourself, 'who is it that I would go to first, who would I think of if it were the last day of man?' then you know for sure who is close to your heart. You see our minds make up the reality around us, we think we know what is happening in our world but realistically our personal version of life and what we are is not the same as the reality that in fact, it is. So who Acmed, who is it you would save?"

Acmed pondered a moment then smiled but before he could speak the assassin spoke again,

"Hold that thought, for that is who you truly love, that is the one, no film star or musician. Remember it's the characters that they play that you love, the image a director gives you, they take on all that you wish to be, they act like you wish to act but that is not the real person underneath. Its the same for musicians, they play and create things you love but that is not a reflection on the person they are, admittedly it would be interesting to talk to some of them, but remember put them in a place where they belong, as a mild point of interest, never idolise something that is not above yourself and in point of fact is usually below you, they may have the money but more often than not they don't have the humility."

The assassin hid his pipe and began to rise,

"Come its time for us to leave, we don't want to be here for the credits, plus it's not my type of film, it did not stir my emotion, it was another CGI-fest that was pointless. Even though cinema has produced a phenomenal amount of wonderful productions in this new era it has also its equal on the opposite scale. Productions of the poorest quality supported by vivid colours and illusions to trick the eyes, this too is false so be careful in what you give your heart to Acmed, make sure it is truly what you love that you give your attention to."

Acmed and the assassin slipped out of the fire exit, leaving the flickering images of the screen to reflect in the eyes of the dead, sat slumped watching the film for eternity.

XVI
DOGMA

A hazy smoke crept up the atmosphere, clinging to each molecule as the beeswax candle spat its miniature ejaculation, a mini-projectile that was chorused by the foaming spittle of the priest's mouth. The assassin sat on the oak wood pew, a dark selection of carvings forged by an ancient hand. The priest was set in the dim candle light robed in scarlet, the mark of blood, blood spilled by a thousand years of war, blood of Christ, the blood of God but above all, the blood of the innocent. The assassin's face was hidden within a deep shadow as Acmed, the apprentice, leaned forward swimming out of the dark overhang. The priest continued his sermon to the deaf, those who attend for the benefit of self-relief. The assassin spoke, a thick treacle mass of words that issued with longevity.

"Dogma, it penetrates the world in all mediums of social interaction, it is the failing of man to avoid change."

Acmed glanced over to the assassin.

"Surely Dogma does not exist in all spheres, what of science and academia, the realms of forward thinking and innovation, where the great minds strive for technological, theoretical and philosophical change?"

"Now my young apprentice, those institutions are among the most corrupt. With dogmatic thought, innovation and revelations are often met with a despising smile and an impenetrable systematic thought process. The fear of rejection from a restricted certified consortium leads to the suppression of experimentation outside of the prescribed formulaic pathways open to the academic. It is only when irrefutable evidence blows open the gates of understanding that a further thread of investigation is accepted and it is these threads that turn in cycles of popularity. No, my friend, this world is not dogma free."

Acmed sat back into the deepening shadow as the priest raged like a beast at the altar, plumes of emotion pouring into the air from the exhausts of his passion, leaving his face a grimace of monstrosity. The assassin spoke again, his eyes never leaving the priest, white highlights in the dark that held a deep knowledge.

"Man has established a ten stage system to dogmatise the world around him, a decahedron of despair, anything that requires a solution in reality follows this system to some extent. The ten stages are: Reality; a problem; the solution to the problem; the acceptance of the solution into common knowledge; the formulisation of this solution; the formula then committed to record; the record then being held as a tradition; the dogmatisation of this system which then leads to the system being assessed or analysed and then finally the abolishment of the system."

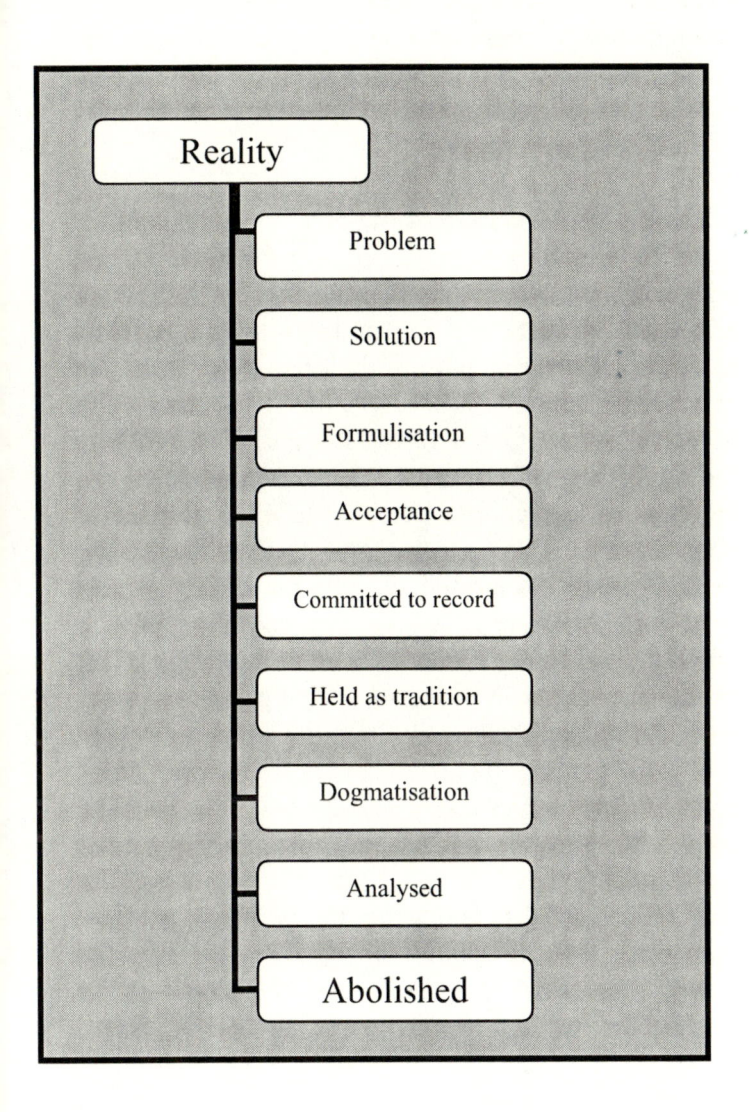

```
Reality
├── Problem
├── Solution
├── Formulisation
├── Acceptance
├── Committed to record
├── Held as tradition
├── Dogmatisation
├── Analysed
└── Abolished
```

Acmed nodded his head as the priest poured the creamy red wine into the goblet upon the altar, a gold chalice that held a thousand reflections of candlelight. The assassin spoke again.

"Take the fiscal system of the modern world, money itself is a prime example of this system. In the beginning man simply lived in *reality*, he felt hunger and cold, he answered the problem with a realistic solution. However, during the transition from the Mesa-lithic period which was an existence of a nomadic nature to the Neo-lithic period which was the beginning of a sedentary existence and saw the addition of agriculture there became a surplus of productivity. This surplus and a decreased time demand upon the individual, plus the ability to now store and accumulate luxury commodities, found a gap for sought-after items. This is the evolution of the ***problem*** stage; man now had luxury goods and tools that allowed an individual to form a status of power. The gold torque, the bladed plough tip and metal tools became increasingly lusted after. The problem came with transport and manufacture. People needed a commodity that was easily transportable as well as still being useful to allow for the purchase of these goods but from this problem we enter the ***solution*** phase. Previously, trade had been the staple of the transaction world, useful items for useful items; however, there came the solution, the ingot! A small half moulded piece of metal that could easily be carried and as it came in various semi finished forms, depending on what the final product was going to be, it was highly sought after and entered the human psyche as a practical *solution* which led it to be *accepted*."

Acmed looked to the priest. A finger of accusation swayed the crowd as the host crumbled in the opposite hand. The assassin continued:

"After this was accepted by the populace, it had to be *formalised*, the ingot became smaller, more compact, easier to trade, have a higher density of metals that had precious value because of the ability to use them in manufacture, and hence the modern coin was established. The mint struck coins at a maximum rate even debasing them by removing percentages of the base metal, removing the real value and imposing a *record* of the coins worth. Images then struck on to the coin would tell the origin and overall sovereign of a realm and in the roman era would help command the loyalty of the troops towards the emperor as opposed to the commander of the army. *Tradition* then follows, remembering that money was a simple form of trade between two people it was then the case that two parties could no longer trade!"

The assassin's voice showed the most uncharacteristic expressions of emotion as his lip curled slightly in a grimace as he said the words, backed by the priests charge and vocal command to heaven as he rose to his sermon. The assassin became poised again and continued.

"No longer can I walk in to Tesco or any supermarket and ask if they would like to take the painting I just finished for a weeks supply of fish. Is there a law that says I cannot barter? Does the government say I will not be able to swap items? No, they do not. It is merely a stupid tradition aided by modern technology that allows two people who would like to exchange the ignorance of their rights. People are trapped in a tradition that makes them believe that money has an intrinsic value when it does not. This tradition has a very fine line and border between its brother, **dogmatisation**. A man can manipulate the value of money, a stock broker or dealer in shares can simply move electronic amounts of money from one imaginary place to another, moving them across the boundary of countries, another man-made concept. This movement generates false interest and false wealth. However, the power of belief, a belief that money has values, gives them wealth unimaginable and they claim it's a risk. A risk to bet electronic valueless units against other valueless units and they call it risk, tell that to the fireman stood in the inferno or the knight running the *Tilt*, risk indeed? Even the simple belief in the bank note is a dogmatisation itself. Bank notes have been found in ancient china and the modern western bank was founded by the Knights Templar in their expansion across the crusade pilgrimage. The note is merely an 'I owe you', that has such a backing by the powerful banks, power gained from false wealth, that its value is 'guaranteed', a guarantee people believe in enough to take paper for gold…paper for gold! That is, until the 'guarantee' fails and then they want much more paper for gold."

The priest showed the audience a wafer and gave it power by his words and asked them to come and drink of the blood of the Christ and to eat his divine flesh.
"I will bring an end to this sermon young apprentice with the fact that money has now been **analysed**, an analysis that is taking place as we speak. Coins are being downsized as their base value does not even cover the cost of the metal to produce it; we have a world of monarchs with their faces on valueless bits of scrap which were once real gold. Cheques are falling from use and being refused by some as out of date and worthless and the percentage of people paying by switch card and electronic forms is getting closer to that 100. I tell you my little *tyro* that money will be gone before you or I are dead."

The assassin moved further back into the darkness of the shadow, as he stood up and excused himself with the politeness and stillness of a seraph. He walked up to the sacred alter and joined the back of the short queue. The priest looked down on his subjects with authority. The assassin took the blessing and handed the cup back to the priest who looked down with a smile. As the two, master and assassin walked from the cathedral the apprentice noticed the assassin place something in his pocket with a crafty hand and asked a question.

"And **abolishment**?" quizzed Acmed

The assassin smiled, "Abolishment, yes the end and annihilation of money. We are in that stage now. With analysis comes the need for reform and as I said money will be gone soon, its abolishment will be complete, but not in a positive way. The real will give way to the electronic and the man dressed in furs giving fish to another man for a leg of meat will truly be dead and his ghost will be a selection of electronic impulses moving around the world as we all do our shopping and banking online."

The two walked off under the eye of the priest, moving down the snowy road until the two were out of sight, lost in a mist of reality and cold, the priest spoke. "He better be worth that sort of money."

XVII
THE ORIGINS OF HUMANS

"What is a human?"
The assassin's voice rang through the wispy rain, encircled by the standing stones. He stood there a sleek dark figure in the dawn of the morning, a morning under the view of the green rolling mountains. Walking around one of the grey monoliths, Acmed spoke back.
"A human is a creature outside of nature that has learnt to overcome its animal instincts."
"True, true. But in the evolution of the world what is a human?"
Acmed pondered and replied,
"Any creature from the *Homo Erectus* family would consist of being human."
"Good, good, yes any of the multiple strains of humanity that have fallen no matter how primitive are in fact human. With that in mind think about humanity as a whole and its concept of itself. We are the last strain of humanity to be alive, we are the last remnants of a species that took millions of years to develop, a species that conquered nature's purpose and place for us and trampolined ourselves to the 'top', whatever that means."
The assassin looked into the grey distance.
"You see Acmed, humans have lived for around six million years as an animal that could be identified as human."
Acmed interrupted,
"I thought it was 3 million years?"

"In fact Acmed, we really don't know, the date and lineage of human evolution, it constantly changes depending on the newest find, but the time itself does not matter, it is the fact that we have existed much longer then we can remember and in many different forms. The key to this lesson is that humans have lived on this earth in one form or another for many times the amount of time that we have. Our great family, our great races have been the masters of this world for millions of years. While nature holds the greatest force, humanity holds the title of master of the world. Anyone who tells you that is untrue and that other creatures are the 'kings of the proverbial jungle' is mistaken. Don't get confused Acmed, humans are the most dangerous animals on the planet, and we are killers, murderers and hunters, a dangerous foe indeed. But we as *Homo- sapiens* are the most deadly of all. If you look at the evolution of man you will see that the world of humans is not the world of humans that we know and 'love'. The world of humans is a selection of tribal societies that have existed and had transition for millions of years, being tempered by the forces of nature to hold their numbers at bay, having a high death rate to keep the sometimes 'virus' of humanity on the doorstep of overpopulation. For 99% of human experience the world of the human has been a symbiotic relationship with the natural world around them. If you could transport a cross-section of all the humans that have ever lived and interview them about the world, 99% of the answers would be about an abundant world that feeds, clothes and keeps them warm, a Garden of Eden if you like."

With this the assassin raised his eyebrows then continued to talk as moisture collected on his clothes and face.

"This Garden of Eden and wonderful landscape is the back setting for the world of humans, a world without taxation, dictators, a distinct lack of murder and violence. A world that even though it has its problems they are problems of survival and not that of man's inhumanity to man. But then of that 100% cross-section you would get the remaining 1% whose understanding of the world was an exponential surge in population, which leads to a loss in the relationship between Mother Nature and humans. No longer does this vast garden supply for its children, now the children overrun it, eating all they can, burning, chopping, destroying everything, creating a false environment to live in, polluting the world, killing their resources. They don't do this as individuals – they are caught up in a worldwide wave of consumerism, from the vast production of the Roman Empire to the fumes of the industrial revolution to the busy streets of dirty Beijing. It's not one person or even a corporate group that is changing humanity it is everybody together not taking a stand and stopping this tide. We could as a world put up a barrier if we wanted, we could unify and stop this destruction of our world. But we don't, we continue to buy plastic, we continue to kill the world."

The assassin stopped as a group of figures, a selection of deeper shadows came through the hazy rain. As they came into view it was clear that they were a group of morning ramblers, enjoying a morning stroll through this ancient site.

"Good morning."
The lead man spoke, "Beautiful morning is it not?"
The group came to a halt, an assemblage of elderly walkers, kitted out in Gortex and modern walking canes, each one in bright clothes and cheerful smiles in craggy faces."
The assassin spoke,
"Good morning to you also sir, a wonderful morning indeed."
The old leader of the group smiled.
"What a lovely site indeed, there is something about the beauty of the unspoilt world that captures the heart of me."
The old man looked to his Rolex and called to the rest.
"Time for a cucumber sandwich and a nice cup of tea I feel."
Then he looked to the assassin,
"Nice to talk to you, we will just rest for a moment, enjoy the stones."
The assassin smiled and nodded as the old man and the group sat on the far side of the stone circle and opened steaming flasks. The assassin walked over to Acmed.
"You see man has existed in a different world to us. We as modern humans only took our place about 35,000 years ago. We are the fingernail of humanity; its very edge but we have either systematically or incidentally destroyed all other humans on this earth. We are the only remains of our vast tree left. The Neanderthal existed for 250,000 years. They lived for a quarter of a million years in the same way. We thought at first that they were dumb stupid animals,

but now we know they had art, language a concept of an afterlife. They were humans as we were, maybe they too would have come along with us on our ride of destruction if they had survived but what we do know is that, even if unintentional, they kept in balance with the world for many times more then what we have even existed. There is no problem with human evolution Acmed, but we as intelligent people should control our world. We should live within nature and have our technology integrated with the world around us. Our society has the simple problem of a high birth rate and a decreased death rate; this is the key to the heart of all problems. What we need to do is make a unified decision to decrease the population; we need to bring it down all across the globe. If we could come to an end of global wars then we would be comfortable in decreasing our populations. With this we would have the technology to support us for a lower cost of living. Couple this with a reintegration into the natural world and its bountiful produce, then we would have a pathway to a utopia. Maybe not the utopia of complete peace but the utopia of a world where people live in balance and do not fight for land or produce, a land where conflict is a conflict of opinion not a conflict of wealth. So remember Acmed, because primitive man did not have the technology that we had that does not make them below us, in all facts they outdo us in relation to the world. Would you give up the plastic blender for the freedom of life in its natural state? The one thing we do not know about our ancient fathers is there philosophy. If they new that they were in balance with the world, if they understood the importance of a world without overpopulation then they are our masters, they are our teachers indeed."

The group of old walkers began to stir from their break and stood up, ready to walk on, ready to explore the world. The leader of this tribe stood and turned to the pair of assassins.

"Have a good day young men, enjoy the sites."

He turned around and began to walk off, but the assassin called after him.

"Nicholas Johnson? You are the head of a set of unified shadow corporations in China, America and Japan."

This was not a question, the old man turned and with a much deeper face said,

"Yes, what do you want?"

The assassin pulled out a gun from his black jacket, the eyes of the quarry sharpened in understanding. Then the sound of hell rang out as the trigger was pulled. Mr Johnson's body erupted as a vile red-black spay of bullet gore splattered across the ancient stones of man. The rest of the group screamed in shock. Mr Johnson's wife fell to her knees and the two assassins melted into the grey cover of the rain.

XVIII
Enlightenment

The smell of rustic bread and flour was complemented by the almost odourless flavour of truly fresh fish. The assassin and Acmed walked from the fishmonger stall with their purchase and lunch. They sat in the bustling traditional market and began to slowly partake of the meal they had. The assassin, taking slow deliberate bites, spoke to Acmed.

"If I was to give you an image of a white light at the end of a very long dark tunnel what situation comes into your mind?"

Acmed responded with a slight laugh as he rocked backwards,

"I take it that this is not a train coming towards me and that I am not tied to the tracks like in some old silent film?"

The assassin finished chewing with ease and whispered,

"No, no, Acmed, quite right. It's not a train, but interesting that you thought of that."

Acmed brought his answer forth with speed and without pause,

"Then it is the image of going to 'heaven' or whatever heaven is for you. It's an out of body spiritual experience."

The assassin looked sideways.

"Good attempt and classic in thought but that is not the situation I was thinking of. A bright light at the end of a dark long tunnel is the experience of enlightenment that a small group of people will achieve."

Acmed looked with a question in his eye.

"A small group? Are you saying that the enlightened few only see a tunnel?"

"Not at all, the small group I'm referring to are the few that actively seek enlightenment, not the enlightened. The enlightened are an immensely select few that reach the light. I think this will be easier if I give you an analogy to work with."

The assassin put down his meal and spoke with his hands in accompaniment.

"Ok, Acmed, imagine a vast pit in the ground, a pit big enough to encompass the souls of all the world's population. Then at a 45 degree angle to this is a tunnel leading upward, a long and vast tunnel. At the end of this tunnel is an opening that reveals a light. All souls, spirits or whatever you wish to call them are housed in the dark pit. This represents the darkness that comes with complete spiritual ignorance. The long and expansive tunnel is the journey towards enlightenment and – of course – the light at the end of the tunnel is enlightenment itself."

Acmed took more of his bread as he listened to the master assassin. They had sat in the centre of the medieval town square next to the market square cross and modern life went on around them.

"Now that we have the image of the spiritual journey in mind we can discuss the individual elements. I said that a small group of people see the tunnel; this is because the vast majority of the masses walk around in the dark searching for nothing. They seek nothing and want for nothing in a spiritual context. But these people are not the idiotic zombies that you are now imagining. These are the majority of the population:

managers, doctors, shopkeepers and all other professions. Your status in life has nothing to do with your spiritual journey. Now in this pit are the idiots of the world, the thieves, organised criminals and all the other dregs of society. They all rub shoulders together. Now these people live in enlightened ignorance because it's not in their mind to move forward out of the pit, in fact they don't realise there is a way out of the pit at all. These people are concentrated on the physical aspects of the world. They are obsessed with consumerism, bodily pleasures and those things that bring immediate feelings of bliss without lasting effects. Are you with me so far?"

Acmed nodded but did not speak.

"Ok then. Now, these people have one good point over me and you, they don't live in dank despair like you would imagine, they actually live in blissful ignorance. They walk in the dark from one distracting pleasure to another never realising there is a way to the light. Now you may feel sorry for these people living lives entirely made up of fleeting pleasures but they have a good life in that they don't struggle spiritually. They are relaxed and unaffected by the rendering effects of spiritual searching. However, even with their blissful dark ignorance they are at the bottom and captured within a distraction. It is a false happiness. The second lot of people are the small group of people on the path to enlightenment. These people are the ones who have started along the tunnel towards illumination. Even though this group is small they encompass 99% of all the people actively searching for enlightenment. This is where the vast majority wonder. However the tunnel defies the logic of physics. This tunnel looks like it is going up, but sometimes you travel down as it shifts allowing you an easier journey. If you run head long at the light you will move no further forward and you will run on an infinite circle forever trying to get to the light, but direct travel will not get you there on this metaphysical journey. The journey towards enlightenment is another lesson but simply understand that the tunnel defies logical thinking and its form changes depending on your path towards enlightenment. However, the people in this tunnel are the worst off. They are the people who have tasted the light. They have lived in the bliss of enlightenment for seconds only. They have tasted the golden honey of true happiness. But this is the problem, they technically live in a tunnel and the tunnel is still dark, it's a dark place but not like the pit. In the pit that is your world, that's all you know. But if you live on the tunnel then you can see everyone else in bliss and ignorance, if you look forward you can see the light at the end but you seldom reach it. Therefore you are left in a dark middle seeing happiness behind you and happiness in front whilst you struggle in the dark to move forward whilst in reality your journey is not a straight line. It is these people who long to either return to blissful ignorance or to be enlightened – but this wish itself takes you away from the moment and the path you are on."

The assassin tore a piece of bread.

"Then there are the third set of people, the ones who have reached the tunnel's edge and who bathe in constant glory; the truly enlightened and the truly happy. However, Acmed I can tell you nothing of these people or this state of mind for I have never been there. Also I have never met an enlightened person. I have met people who claim to be but it's obvious that they are not: they can disguise it well but its untrue. I'm afraid I can tell you no more on that subject."

Acmed looked slightly disappointed and the assassin continued quickly.

"However, Acmed, there is another dimension to this story. The light at the end of the tunnel is not a fixed constant. You must view this light like the sun, it moves in orbit, it shifts and as a result its light hits different parts of the tunnel. For example, the people in the pit, in their darkness are not people who never experience the effects of enlightenment, occasionally the light passes down the tunnel and hits the pit, those in the range of the light are representative of those people on earth who have a moment of true bliss for no reason, they feel as light as air and don't know why, this is when their mind opens up to true happiness but just as it came it goes again, quickly to be replaced by the search for false happiness. The same goes for those in the tunnel, they are closer to the light and are in its direct view, they are actively looking for where the light will land and thus can find those moments of true happiness more often then others. The aim of the game is to spend 24 hours a day in the light. But you see Acmed this is where most people get it wrong, they think enlightenment is like a flash in the dark and then, in one second you have enlightenment. This does happen sometimes but for most of us it's a search for the light, it's a search for fleeting moments. It is our goal to try to get as many of those as we can, letting the amount build up until we live in the light. As I said though, I have never been enlightened, Acmed."

The assassin looked thoughtful.

"There was only once for me Acmed, just once and it was at the height of my martial training. I had just read a fantastic book about this subject and I walked to the local shop, I smelt fresh fish and I bought some bread, it was at that moment I had about 40 seconds of true enlightenment then as it came it went and left me with a longing, a feeling of emptiness."

They both looked to the bread in their hands and the assassin commented.

"I do try to recreate that feeling but I realise now that I don't need to recreate it, that I can't recreate it, I need to open myself up. But I do like the fish and bread due to the feeling it gives me now."

They both looked up at the sun and took in the smells of the market.

XIX
THE MARTIAL ARTS

Spikes of black and jade thrust themselves out of the snow, trees that bent under the burden of the snow. The grove encompassed two figures dressed in black, a pale moon hung in a sparkling sky and the wind was constant but kind. The Master assassin was instructing the arts of war to his apprentice. Each time the apprentice attempted a strike his body would make a new pattern in the snow as he was thrown through the air or forced to his knees under a painful lock. As time passed the two took a break and sat in the centre of the white grove to talk. The assassin looked at Acmed and Acmed looked to the assassin, both with eyes of haunted steel, looking but saying nothing, smiling but not laughing, the bond of true brothers, brothers in arms in the true sense of the word.

The assassin spoke into the wind, "The Martial arts, the arts of war, a stream of knowledge that has been passed down for generations in all cultures, from Tibet to China, from the Celts and Anglo-Saxons to the Vikings; all of these nations had the martial arts. Martial knowledge has existed in all cultures. It was even still evident in Victorian England in the form of Single Stick fighting. It's only recently, within the last four or five generations, that the martial arts in the West has all but died out. Its current revival in the form of Asian martial arts is the most recent story in a set of traditions that go back to the dawn of man. But no matter what the martial art and no matter what the style there is one fundamental element that all marital arts require."

The assassin looked at Acmed for an answer, a slight cock of the head. Acmed looked to the moon and thought out load.

"Determination?"

The assassin corrected,

"Discipline and determination."

There was a pause in the air before the assassin continued.

"All martial arts require discipline and determination. Now when I speak of martial artists I will have to clarify what I mean. By martial artist I don't mean a thug who can naturally fight and has been gifted with the ability to kill. I mean the person who seriously pursues the martial way, the way of skill, someone who follows a code of ethics and persists in making his body and mind unified and attempts to perfect this unity. This is a martial artist and I don't mean the fat guy who trains twice a week at his local club then goes for six pints of beer afterwards and collects all the magazines and DVDs he can."

"Master, where is the cut off point between Martial artist and imitator?"

"Look at it this way Acmed. If you spend more time thinking about perfecting your martial abilities then actually perfecting them then you are on the wrong path. If you know in your heart that you are reaching for perfection then you are on the correct path but actually having the skill is only a by-product of the martial way of life. The martial arts give you discipline and determination: two much needed qualities in this life. In the past you would have been a warrior, a farmer, a craftsman, a scholar or leader and usually you were a mixture. Each of these disciplines has one thing in common; they all require discipline and determination. If you did not plant, you would starve; if you did not make, you could not sell; if you did not learn then knowledge ended; if you did not lead then the tribe would die. Now, in today's world, all of these things have been taken away from the people. The soldiers launch their weapons from space, the farmer relies upon machines, the machine replaces the craftsman, the scholar has been replaced by the Internet and TV and the leaders are usually a group of corrupt individuals that lead the country to failure. Once a leader does not have contact with the people he is leading then true leadership is replaced by dictatorship under the guise of democracy. My grandfather told me that it would only take one honest man to lead this country correctly, and I would bow down to the dictatorship of one honest man as opposed to being ruled in a corrupt democracy."

The assassin centred his speech,

"Ok, now that we have replaced those things that give us determination and discipline we have created a generation of soft, unruly people who understand only that they can manipulate the system and have no ethical code to teach them that this is disrespectful to themselves. The governmental aid systems are in place to help the weak, but as people have no ethics they pretend to be weak in order to gain aid. If these people would have had a martial upbringing then they would prefer to die then to get aid undeserving. Through the martial arts is born the strength of a nation. We look back to history and celebrate the warlike nations, the Samurai, the Vikings, the Celts; all of these people hold a vast respect, and why? Because they were nations who sought war? No, not at all. They are respected because they hold the tales of individuals who are brave, disciplined and have no fear to live life to the full and have no fear of life itself. They don't try to sneak in and get help for nothing, they are proud people who lived life as it should be lived."

The assassin gave a short pause as he collected his thoughts.

"You see Acmed, we need to get the youth of our nation and take them by the hand and lead them forward. We have created about three generations of people who are largely worthless in truth. Trying to teach children discipline and determination through lectures or other such means is useless. What they need is an outlet for their energy, an outlet that can quell their aggression and at the same time give them the correct lessons they need. Of course men will always fight, there will always be trouble, but those same war-like men who grew up with a martial background will help that old lady across the road, go over to the car accident and give aid, stop the man hitting his girlfriend in a drunken rage. These are the things he would do, but what does our generation do instead? They rob the old women, laugh at the crash or take joy in the macabre vision as they stand and watch the girl get hit because to get involved will end up with a night in prison or maybe dead. We have created a weak nation of people who are insular with no central discipline. The reality of brave and true war has been taken away. The reality of survival in this world has been removed. We are left with a nation of people who follow and do not think, without any capability to think on their feet – all aspects that a martial life will give you."

The assassin and Acmed sat in the lunar silence for a moment, and then Acmed spoke

"So you think that it is the job of all parents to find the correct way to instil ethics into their child and not only that but also discipline and determination?"

"I do Acmed. But I also think that we should make our people a martial people again. We were once a nation famed for fighting skill; other nations would tremble at the English, the Empire. The English man was a proud man with sword in hand ready to fight for monarch and country never wanting any white feathers. Now we are a nation without identity. A nation of women for men who care too much about fashion and we have women who are men, overweight binge drinkers that swear like troopers, the English lady has died. What we need is a national martial arts system that has a nation wide curriculum that will be taught in schools and entered into the education system. We could then regulate it and teach our people to be warriors again. In twenty years we would have a new generation of disciplined people who could all fight and be ready for war if the country needed them. Imagine adding to that curriculum basic army training spread over the school period. Instead of a standing army you would have a 'standing nation' of men and women ready for war and ready to help each other; a union of power and respect."

XX
SUICIDE

The man looked up from his desk as the assassin's silenced gun looked back at him.
"So you are here to top me off then?"
The assassin nodded with a slight inclination and the man looked about the room calmly and with a logical gaze.
"There is no way out for me is there, Mr Assassin?"
"No, I'm afraid there is not."
"Well then, Master Assassin, would you mind if I take my own life as opposed to you doing the deed for me?"
The man was calm and the realisation of his end seemed to be an inevitability to him.
"In what manner would you like your end to be?"
The man said calmly,
"I would like to hang myself so that my body may go onward to the afterlife without the destruction that a bullet would bring – however, as I am Catholic, I would like you to kick the chair out from under me as to avoid the damnation of suicide."
The assassin nodded to Acmed and asked for rope. Acmed, dressed in black, reached into his bag and found some climbers' rope, placing it on the desk next to the target's hands. The man looked at the rope and to the master assassin.
"Do you mind if I take a few moments in prayer?"
"Where?"

The man looked over to the corner of the room, to a table with a medieval folding icon sitting on top.
"Acmed."
Acmed knew his job. He searched the corner well, checking for weapons.
"It's clean."
The assassin looked to the man,
"Make peace with the maker."
The man stood up, broad and flat faced, a hard man. He walked over to the corner, knelt and began to pray. The two assassins watched in silence as he began. Within a moment he turned round.
"The silence is not welcome, please you may talk, talk so I may have solitude in my prayer."
The assassin turned to Acmed and asked,
"What do you think of suicide? Apart from in this case, I may say now that this is a noble death, what I am asking about is the normal situation and event that we call suicide."
Acmed sat in a chair, his gun aimed at the kneeling man.
"I think suicide has its place. I think that if a human has gone beyond the realms of normality, if they have committed actions that have been so foul that they cannot atone for it in any way, no matter what they do. If they have explored all ways and none of them will suffice then I think suicide is a noble end. If say, your death would benefit others, for example rushing headlong in to battle knowing that it is a certain death but your actions result in a greater good then that too is noble. But on the other hand if that concept is perverted, like Edo period *Seppuku* in Japan – the

concept of ritual disembowelment – then it is a flawed thing."
"Why Edo period?"
"You see Master, Japanese Hara-kiri was invented for those situations when all was lost and it would be better to die then to live on. But as it became dogmatised as a ritual, then people asked for it for fewer and fewer substantive reasons. It got to the point where it was outlawed because it was getting out of hand. As for the rest of suicide, the average suicide in life is due to a weakness in character."
The assassin butted in,
"Why so?"
"You see Master; a person commits suicide because they can see no other way out of the grimness of their own existence. This must mean that they cannot see the beauty in life. Natural beauty stands all around us, the gateway to happiness is simply a state of mind, if you learn how to switch happiness on then your existence becomes wonderful. For example, some people commit suicide because of massive losses on business deals, they kill themselves because they have lost money. They don't do this because they have made a mistake and wish to apologise to everybody for their folly. They do it because it has bankrupted them and people that rich usually consider money as life. Without money and the lifestyle they lead they perceive themselves as dead anyway. If this was a true way then all tramps would commit suicide, those who lose on a business transaction still have more then a tramp, yet some tramps are happy with that existence. There are millions of poor people in third world countries who

have nothing yet still smile. So money is not the issue, the issue is they cannot eradicate the unhappiness from their minds. They see riches as happiness so without happiness life is grim and unbearable. Therefore they end it. A complete lack of character."

"Very good Acmed, anything else?"

"Yes there is, I think that this lack of character comes from weak parents producing weak children. We don't teach kids anything about strength and honour and the value of life. When there is no love of live there is no respect for it. People used to have a firm belief that if you killed yourself then you would go to a worse place then the one you are in now, but now that the church is dying and its ethics gone we see the afterlife as blank nothing. It is irrelevant if it is true or not, what is important is that people believed that they had it better here then if they committed suicide, therefore they should try to find a way to make improvements in their lives. You see Master, for those people who are suicidal I would say this. Life may be shit, you may be at the lowest ebb and you may be in a position that is disagreeable. But know this: no matter what situation you are in there is always happiness to be found. The best things in life are free, they truly are. Nature is full of marvels; just take a look around you at the world you are in. Even if you are a slave or captive there is always something to find happiness in. Even if you are away from the natural world you have the limitless world of the mind. The vast forests of mystery that exist inside, you can write a great poem, an epic story or even write a book on radical philosophy. Train your mind to remember, and if there is no way to record your thoughts – train your mind to become a master of oral transmission. The ancients of Homer's time would recite vast tombs by rhyme and measure. Teach yourself to be a true human. If you are killing yourself out of love then you are weak, everybody should be a true happy individual with or without a loved one. A relationship is about two people engaging their lives not sharing them. If you disengage then you should return to your happy state and continue to enjoy your existence on your own. If you are living in a first world country or have the means to a normal or standard life then learn to paint, learn the great arts, mathematics, geometry and all those things which make men great. If you are suicidal turn your depression into an inquisition, question the world around you, look at the great mysteries of life, spend your waking life aiming for perfection, you will find that as you search harder and harder you will leave despair behind and raise up to happiness, even if you never answer anything. One of the greatest tools of the mind is conscious decision. If you have a problem that you are suicidal about and it's a problem that you cannot resolve or it is out of your control, then you must use a failsafe. Every time that situation comes into your head, every time that you begin to role play your woe in your mind say 'stop!'. Tell yourself that you are dwelling on the negative, creating a rotten mind, and then change the subject of your thoughts. You will return to your woes every few minutes but be strong with yourself, in your mind's eye shout, be the teacher that tells you off. Eventually as you become more disciplined and keep them thoughts out, nicer thoughts will creep in, until the woes of your life only come occasionally."

Acmed looked like he had finished and he sat back. Now the condemned man looked to the assassin and spoke,
"I am finished and I am grateful that the words I heard at the end of my life were as profound as they were. Thank you both for your cooperation. Master assassin, you do indeed have a true and noble pupil, I wish you both happy lives and I forgive you my death, it is my fault that you have been hired and I am glad that it was you and not some thug in the dark. Indeed I am truly humbled."
With that he gave a nod and placed the rope over a beam. As he prepared for his death he said a prayer and stood on a chair. He took a moment then nodded to the assassin. With the kick he began to choke, within minutes his life ended and the two assassins closed the door on his office as they left.

XXI
War

The thatched hut was deep in Devonshire countryside. An orange inferno pulsated from the dark door as the sword-smith worked late at night, forming a knife blade in the old ways with the twists of pattern-wielding, foreboding patterns in iron beneath an English moon. The sparks flew in chorus with each hammer stroke and the two assassins sat in the corner, watching the working of Acmed's new assassin's tool.

"Acmed, tonight you become an assassin in truth. You have completed your training with me. Now you will be given the ritual blade of our order, an order of a very select few that goes back centuries. After this evening you will be a complete adept and yet you will work with me until I retire, which is not old in our profession."

A smile.

"Tonight you will become my equal in status but I will remain your Master, a Master of war."

The assassin looked deep into the flames as the smith and his assistant worked their magic. This was a craft the assassin admired. The assistant plunged the bellows and the master hammered away. The assassin came from his trance with a mild recognition.

"War, Acmed, war. The reality of human existence, the factor that has accompanied us like a wraith through time, war and destruction. Did you know that, in the Mesolithic and through to the Neolithic there is literally only a tiny amount of evidence for war. I know that evidence itself for lots of early human existence is scarce, and that just because the evidence is not there then it does not mean that it did not happen. However, I feel that this tiny amount of war represents the truth of the matter, where there are less people and more land there is bound to be less war, it only follows common sense. But what I want to talk to you about tonight is the art of war but when I say war I want to clarify what I mean. By war I mean the clash of armies without modern weapons. "The definition of true war for me is military men or men ordained in the martial ways clashing together, without the aid of modern ballistic weapons. A situation where men can prove their worth on the field of battle and the chance of survival is in their hands and not in the hands of fate and random bullet trajectories. The way of steel and the way of the warrior, not the carpet bombing of innocents in holy places."

Acmed looked attentively at the illuminated face of his master as he continued his lesson.

"First let me say this Acmed, I think a world without war and humans that live in self regulated low populations is the ultimate utopia and this is the dream of any civilised man. However, this dream is still a dream and is a far cry from the world that we live in now. So whilst the world is rife with war there is a need for warriors but we, as a race, have taken war to extremes – extremes that have taken away the concept of chivalry. But in real war, the war of the ancients I mean, there are positive sides that complement the negative. In the old ways there was a balance that war gave and this is what I want to talk to you about tonight."

Acmed kept his attention focused.

"You see war had positive aspects that we don't think about. Firstly war is the ultimate glue that binds communities together. With the threat of the tribes of neighbouring peoples coming over the hill you feel strength in numbers and you rely on the community sticking together as a whole. With this tight knitting in place you would need for visual identities, art, literature, oral histories and all the elements that make a community have an identity, all these things come from staying together for survival."

The sword-smith lifted the knife to the light, a sleek and wicked blade with a hellish straight edge that screamed efficiency. He placed it down again and struck the blade again.

"Furthermore, Acmed, war created healthy individuals. If your warrior class were unfit and incapable there were no forms you could fill in and claim benefits. You could rarely appeal to a higher government for aid and you could not rely on someone else to fix the problem. You had to have fit fighting men who were peak athletes that were schooled and disciplined in war; you needed the natural leaders to come forward and take you to victory. Alongside these craftspeople of conflict you needed artisans of the tools of conflict, this brought the need for people to display their creativity and ingenuity, the people at street level were skilled, they had a skill that could be passed on and with skill comes knowledge and with knowledge comes civility. If those idiots on the streets today were highly skilled people there would be less trouble, for each one would be a deeper thinker and have their efforts and energy in other places. It has been said that there is more conflict in peacetime then in wartime. In war people unite and fight a common enemy, in peacetime they fall apart and fight each other, probably because we seek strife as opposed to living in peace. In reality I don't know the people in the other community but I have to live with those around me, therefore I would prefer to live in peace with my own people and at war with others instead of at war with my own and in harmony with others. The problem we have now is that war is on a world scale and at such a destructive level that these positive sides are replaced with, how can I say…hell."

As the assassin said the word the bellows flared up and the room grew in illumination. A slight pause was had as the assassin watched but then he continued.

"Of course there is the factor of natural selection as well. I think you would have to be a Martian to not agree that the human gene pool is at its worst state. We are a weak and pathetic species in comparison to our forefathers. We are a world of the disabled, the retarded, the diabetic, the cancerous, the mentally disrupted and all the other afflictions that curse the human race. We brain wash people into thinking that being disabled is not an issue and it's beautiful to be big; this is utter shit. These people die in nature for a reason, it's because they cannot survive. If you do not even have a chance at survival in the 'real' world outside of modern support then it's not natural to be alive. Yes as higher beings we should look after the weak and we should support the unfortunate but we should not actively continue the existence of someone who is so beyond survival. As harsh as it may sound, the human race is in evolution and it's only logical that what we are doing is harming the natural process. We should help those who can recover and function in society; if these people can contribute in any way, perhaps to science or philosophy, then there is reason to help them. I am as heart broken as the next man at their condition but we have to think of the community, not the individual. It is exactly that self-centred thought that is causing all our problems. In natural life, the way we were meant to live it, war and natural selection would eradicate these elements. But statements like this make the 'do-gooders' cry out NAZI! But they would be the first people to run if war threatened. By not trimming the human race and cutting away the rot we are letting it ferment into a stagnant mass. We are over-populated and we stink. While we are living in other people's pockets there will be conflict, but the result of that conflict is no longer settled with honour or with the strength and skill of the arm. We do live in hell, we truly do."

Again the fire stoked and the smith looked demonic as he pounded away on his anvil. The two of them watched in silence for hours as the smith perfected the weapon, cooled and polished the edge, bound the handle and made the sleek scabbard. They waited until the knife was complete. The smith presented the blade with his apprentice at his side; the assassin with his protégé stood and received it with grace.

"Well done, Master Smith. The relationship between our two orders has existed for countless generations. Thank you for this gift."

The assassin and Acmed walked out into the night and on to high ceremony. By the morning Acmed would be an ordained killer.

XXII
SAFETY TICKET

The boys and girls were spilling laughter into the air as they splashed into the river, each one of them wet and sparkling in the mid-summer sun, enjoying the freedom of childhood. The assassins watched as they played in innocence, small arguments and frivolity, the beauty of youth. As time passed on the joy was interrupted by a firm voice.
"Hey! You children, out now!"
The policeman was escorted by a women; the complaint had obviously come from her.
"Come on out of the water, don't you know it is dangerous? People die in rivers, you could drown!"
The children bled their happiness into the grey aura the adults brought. They climbed the bank and listened to the reprimanding police offer.
"Acmed, how many children die in rivers per year, in your estimation?"
Acmed looked to the assassin, sat next to him under the old oak tree,
"I don't know but I don't think it can be that many."
"No, it's not. Not compared to the fatality rate of car crashes, domestic violence and the damages by other things such as passive smoking."
Acmed nodded as the assassin continued,
"You see Acmed it is this reason, at this generation, that we are creating a nation of wimps. Yes sure some kids die in rivers, but how many millions have the sweet memories of those summer days, how many

remember those long afternoons? Not only that but they learn the environment of open water, they learn their strengths and their limits, without those few sacrifices there is a generation of inexperienced weaklings. To be honest, if those kids died because they could not fight the environment then they put themselves in too much danger. People don't realise that kids are not stupid, but are adults without experience. They are not daft and we as adults are taking away their meaningful experiences. If those kids died then their parents should have taught them better and if it was a situation outside of their control then it was probably meant that they should die that day. It could as easily be a fall from a swing."

The kids were gathering their things and going home, heads down and browbeaten. The woman looked pleased with the result of her complaint and the officer looked on and said,

"Your parents should be ashamed."

The assassin added to his sentence,

"They should be ashamed of not being here to watch over them, that is all officer. You see, Acmed, if we fear for our child's life then we should not stop their education in the real world we should look out for them, in case they get into a situation they cannot handle. The main point I'm trying to give you today is this: life does not come with a safety ticket; there is no official documentation that you receive when you are born. None of us has any guarantee that says '*I give you the right to a healthy 80 year life*'. This ticket never arrives but people of this generation have the idea that they are owed something by someone. We have adopted the American culture of sueing people. Apparently if the pavement has a drop in it of a specific size and you trip over it you can sue, furthermore if you slip on a shop floor that is wet you can sue the shop. What utter shite. Who said anything about having the right to walk on a perfect flat surface or having the right to travel along a dry surface? It sounds insane to me."

The children had all gone, as had the joy in the air. Left over was the quiet sound of nothing, next to the sign that said 'no swimming', ripples on nothing.

"It is the constant onslaught of television advertisements that offer you money for accidents at work, telling you how people can sue for an accident. The word itself should be a clue. So what if you fell off a ladder, if you had made sure it is safe then it is clearly your fault. So what if you trip over a box in the factory, why don't you open your eyes, if you don't notice the box then how do you walk around in a city centre without dying. All these people who talk about, 'the pole was sticking out' or giving in to stupid risk assessments – what a load of tosh."

The assassin seemed quite annoyed and Acmed ventured a thought.

"What about actual dangerous working environments?"

The assassin was quick to respond

"Now that is the key to all this: what is a dangerous environment? For me a dangerous environment is somewhere where you feel that you do not have the ability to conduct yourself in safety. It is where you assess the situation and say, no I'm not confident about this. It is here that the rule should work. If you say to your employer that you don't feel that you can do it and they do not sort you out a safer environment, then that is the real issue of the law. That law is for people who are made to work in an environment that they are not safe in. The world is a dangerous place, it is full of hazards, and life is about damage reduction, not damage avoidance. It is inevitable that the human body will sustain damage, as a person you have to analyse how to get the minimum amount with the least after effects. Having a wet floor is not a dangerous environment."

Acmed spoke again,

"Some people say that we are heading to a world where the risk is being removed, making a safer environment, calming the planet and living in a place of minimum damage. What would you say to them?"

"I would probably shoot them in the face. The planet cannot be tamed; we are living in a dream if we think it can. Even if we took away all the risks what are we achieving but only to nullify the mind? It is danger that keeps you on edge. Be careful with my words though. I do not mean the dangers of man versus man, those are hellish dangers. People should be safe from other people. However, we should not be 100% safe from Mother Nature; it is this natural danger that gives us our drive. It is the ease of living in a first world country that creates the decay of the magnificence of the human engine. We fall over and break our bones, simply from falling over, like a child we should roll with it, get up and laugh and for those people who think that it is age that makes falling hurt they should talk to a stunt man. They should also visit Japan; I have seen the elderly there that can out perform the best of our children. It has nothing to do with race but all to do with the limits we strive for. Here in England we try to take all we can, eat all we can and think of no-one else but ourselves."

The assassin sat back, seemingly pissed off with life. After a few moments Acmed asked, what would the assassin do to change things? With a renewed dignity the assassin spoke.

"I would call for the law of common sense, the process of working out the individual circumstances. But as for the culture of England I would say this. Each and every child should climb a hundred trees swim across a thousand rivers and climb the highest hills they can. Build a fire, own a knife, make a bow and arrow and learn how to survive in the wild. I think as a section of physical education at school they should learn wilderness survival. Imagine a nation of hardy people who can survive outside of the false environment that we have built and image that even the weakest among us could climb mountains and swim lakes. England would call itself proud again, we may have no money, we may have no empire, we have had this taken from us but what nobody can take is the power of faith, not religious faith but the faith in the strong, the faith in the gentleman and the faith that we are no longer a weak race!"

The assassin and the apprentice sat and discussed the problems with Her Majesty's Territory and the weak vein of folk who now inhabit that island. As they spoke small faces appeared at the tree line. The faces became bodies, and the figures of the children crept back to the edge of the pool. Then with a sly cunning they all jumped back into the river, defiant of the unnatural restraint placed on them by folk who should know better!

XXIII
Materialism

"Do you think that a dog would care if he urinated on the Mona Lisa?"
"What!?" came the apprentice's astonished reply.
The assassin continued as he pointed to a dog that was urinating on a lamppost,
"Do you think that a dog would care if he pissed on the Mona Lisa?"
The apprentice replied with sarcasm,
"No I'm sure that he would not."
The assassin adopted the teacher pose.
"You see, Acmed, the dog has not got the concept of material value, he sees it as a target for marking his territory. To the dog a filthy old bone has more use then a few swirls on an old piece of canvas."
Acmed paused for thought and then replied,
"I see what you are driving at but a dog is not a human and only a human can understand the value of art."
The master assassin smirked,
"The value of art? The value of art is dependent on the world around it. When that great master painted that masterpiece it was worth nothing, zero. It's true that old masters painted over their canvas many times because they could not afford to buy more material. They simply painted over 'priceless' pieces of art."
The apprentice interrupted,
"That's because they were unknown, they had not made a name for themselves."
The assassin's finger shot up in triumph,

"That's my point exactly. If the value of the painting was inherent in the fabric of the art then its value would be there the second that the brush hit the canvas. However, that simply is not the case. Value only came to the Mona Lisa when time turned into history and history turned into legend. I could go into any antique art shop and pay a few hundred pounds for something of better skill. The difference is that the world we live in has created a star of that art and its master, and human beings have put value on fame and public awareness. If you put any other painting in the media time and time again and day after day its fame would grow as would its worth. Humans control the value of all things."

The assassin walked past the dog whose eyes sparkled with want of attention. Acmed shot a response as they walked on,

"In your theory then, only water, shelter, food and fire have any worth. If you follow through with your hypothesis."

The journey took them to the posh end of London, with its fashion boutiques and top-notch jewellery shops, where the assassin replied.

"How much is a glass of water worth?"

Acmed pondered the answer,

"Well if you use only the glass as a container and don't add its base cost, a glass of water is worth nothing – zero." The apprentice smiled, satisfied, awaiting a response.

"True, water has no value. But what if that water was for sale in the dessert, one glass for sale to a thousand travellers who had been in the open sun for three days, how much then?"

The assassin slowly added his comments,
"The price of the highest bidder, surely?"
"So, Acmed, if the highest bidder owned the Mona Lisa would he swap it for a single glass of water?"
Acmed replied,
"Yes, if he needed it he would."
The assassin clapped once,
"So, if water has no value then neither does the Mona Lisa, if you follow your logic?"
Acmed smiled at the trap,
"Yes, it has no value."
The assassin continued,
"You see, the world is obsessed with materialism – we love 'stuff'. They say you have to have 'stuff'. While water, shelter, fire and food are available and within your means, society gives people a disposable income. People have given to money a value, a worth, even though it is worthless. So, they need to create other worthless objects to spend that worthless currency on."
Acmed frowned,
So, what would you do, burn all the things that do not sustain you?"
"God no, boy, not at all. To me art is priceless but I mean in the true sense of the word. It has no monetary value; its value is a window to emotion and a doorway to the past. Art and other such 'stuff' is for the nation to see and, young one, I would not wish to destroy it. I know you can't change the world we live in; people will always put a value on stupid things for stupid prices. What I am saying is that you, yourself, should look to your life and only buy what is of real value to you. Food, water, shelter and some forms of

entertainment are needed. As our world has turned from a creative world to a capitalist consumer hell, you should stop yourself from being the extreme consumer. Consumerism is a luxury, you should create 90% of what you need yourself – it's free anyway. Plant some food, raise animals, make your needs fulfilled with creativity. People are so bored because they have nothing to do in this world, no purpose. You must give yourself purpose to stop from filling that boredom with shopping. Shopping and consumerism are not the answers to boredom. Creativity, human ingenuity and fulfilling those lifelong hopes and dreams are the true goals of the human. If a product, like a DVD, a book, art or music stimulates your imagination then it has worth, it has value. Books and knowledge are worth the most; how much would our desert travellers pay for a 'desert survival guide'?"

Acmed laughed, and splattered out,

"Oh yes, that would be worth all the tea in China."

The assassin smiled.

"Remember Acmed, put true meaning and value on objects, do not let society tell you what to pay. A new DVD is worth more then an old one, and why? Because it is more desirable. It is wanted more. The more something is wanted, the higher the cost. Be careful with your life. It's yours, so do not waste it shopping and paying for shiny rocks and soft metal, just because you think it is what you need. What you need is truly different. You need love, experience, safety, joy and sustenance. That is all."

Acmed spoke.

"We are here."

The assassin smiled as he looked at the expensive jewellery shop.
"Shining rocks and soft metal."
The pair opened the door to a fat shop-keep, hideous to the eye from the start.
"Can I help you, gentlemen?"
The assassin pulled out a silenced pistol.
"You should learn the value of paying your debts."
The gun gave a thud. Lesson learned.

XXIV
Politics

The queue was long, hordes of people waiting to vote. The master and the apprentice stood in line, waiting in silence. That was until Acmed broke it.
"Do you think that it's worth voting, Master?"
"That's a difficult question. Is it worth voting? Possibly, yes. Is voting a good way of doing things? No."
Acmed looked surprised.
"I thought you of all people would extend the power of the vote, power to the people?"
The assassin looked quizzical for a moment and then spoke with a slated tone,
"Do you really think that voting is power?"
Acmed replied with schoolboy repetition,
"Democracy is freedom; it's the power of the people."
To which the assassin smiled and said,
"That is wrong, we only hold one power, that is the power to choose between two demons. We choose who we think is best and we hope to get the least terrible one. If we wanted to, we could choose a third or completely different and new faction to rule. But for that, two things need to happen:

Creating a 'real democracy'

> 1. We set up a communication system that would allow us to talk to one another directly, so we can collectively aim all our votes to one place.
> 2. Secondly, we would need a new political party with a radical new look that benefited the populace and that party would need to have funds to advertise themselves, for politics is nothing more then the battle between two powerfully rich factions."

With that the assassin stopped and an old woman in front of him lifted her eyes in a quizzical look. As this happened, Acmed probed the assassin as the queue shuffled along at slow speed.

"So you think there is very little difference in the two major parties?"

"There was once. When they first formed there was a difference. One of them formed as a response to the degradation of the other. It's the same the world over; one party will erect itself to try to beat the injustice of the other. However, after a while, like religion, power seekers move in, people from the upper classes, they move in to take a hold. With that hold they allow others in, once they have a firm hold the politics of the party start to change. They change from their original ethos and adopt a more corruptive stance."

The old woman in front of them started to look at her voting card in contemplation. She began to ponder as the line edged forward and the assassin continued.

"What is really needed is a line of communication to the populace, a way to show them that the truth is different to what they believe."

Acmed flipped a reply,
"Maybe someone should write a book about our conversations."
The assassin smiled.
"That would be one way to tell the populace about the mess it is in."
They both smiled as the queue shortened and the master assassin continued his lesson.
"Most politicians make rules that do not affect them. They pass votes on issues that they themselves will not feel the effect of. It's one rule for one and one rule for another. They pass bills on stopping people building eco-homes, load you with regulations that are ridiculous, but do they have trouble with it? No, they simply have enough money to pay what they need, while those who do not have enough money are ruled by their laws and regulations. Even though there are practical and safe ways around these laws it's the lower classes that suffer because of those who have the means of ruling over them."
The old woman in front looked at the political ribbon upon her chest and thought very deeply to herself.
Acmed gazed around as he spoke.
"If that's the case then I think that there should be one governing law of common sense. It should be the primary law of the law system, if a law goes against common sense and the situation then it should be ruled out and the verdict be innocent."
The assassin added,
"I think that we should go further then that. I think that we should do one of two things: we should either get rid of the government as it is now and have an internet system for voting on each law; we should

have basic laws, plus the common sense law, and then as a nation we should vote on the peripheral laws that affect us."

"And secondly?" asked Acmed.

"Secondly, we should instead have the ability to vote for a panel of experts in each field – for example a panel of academics should have the power to influence or directly change educational laws and it is we, the people, who should vote for these academics. This should be done for each area of life and the most qualified people should make the decisions and we should decide on them."

The old woman unbuttoned her political ribbon as the queue got shorter. The assassin continued.

"We have the ability to let everybody vote on every subject, as long as there is no corruption in the organisation and counting of the votes then all should be fine. The only issue that would arise is when the populace vote outside of common sense, if they voted against a law for individual profit as opposed to the good of the nation."

Acmed redirected the conversation,

"Ok, that is well and good and I see your point but do you think politics is a worthwhile subject?"

The assassin grinned tightly,

"I think politics is the most useless of all the subjects and philosophies. It is the one that affects us the most, but it is the philosophy that is based on hollow grounds – it has no meaning. Would you like me to give you a true rendition of politics?

Acmed nodded and the woman shuffled further as see strained to listen to them. The assassin raised his voice just slightly.

"Ok, it's like this and believe me, it's this simple. Powerful men with big weapons subjugate the weaker ones, sometimes with chivalry and protection in mind and sometimes with corruption. These men then lead. They decide things and set laws. Power moves between factions and powerful men lead the factions and the populace has no choice but to be lead by them: it's that or face charges of treason. Nothing changes until men with bigger weapons come and all of those laws and edicts that were so high and mighty fall and are crippled overnight, meaningless, meaningless under the threat of the new weapons. This power shift still goes on in the world, but here in England we have not had this type of political move for a long time. The same happens in America. They have had their independence and their civil war but who now has the money to form an army, maybe Mr Bill Gates? Maybe he could train an army and introduce his own politics. Because all politics is meaningless and restrictive, it's no longer for the good of the population. Most tax is spent on the worthless: the fat, the smokers and the dregs of humanity, giving them what they can't get themselves. Now Acmed, think on this: imagine some of the British troops are royal, and some of them are not, they are for the government. What would happen if the queen wanted her power back? That's when you would see true politics at work."

The old woman got to the front of the queue and pushed her political ribbon into the bin at the side of the table. She picked up a card and put a cross in a box. The box said, 'None of the above'.

XXV
ZEN AND MEDITATION

The archer and the master were performing an ancient rite. At one end of the *Dojo* was an archer, Japanese, dressed in black and white. At the other was a small old man, dressed in the same *Hakama,* wide black trousers and a white *Gi* top. The assassin and Acmed were the only other two people in this ancient building, both were sat on straw mats. The old master gave a nod and the archer drew back his bow, there was a silence in the air and the sound of leaves on the wind filtered through the room. Then with a sonic snap the arrow was loosed. Acmed's eyes tried to follow but when they arrived at the arrow he found it still, caught in the master's grip. The master and the archer exchanged places. The master then spoke to the archer in Japanese.

"If you catch ten arrows you will be the next master of this school."

With that the Japanese master drew the bow, counting quietly and solidly,

"*Itchi.*"

After a second of silence and pause the arrow loosed and the adept caught it with ease.

"Acmed, what do you think of Zen and meditation?"

Acmed looked with embarrassed surprise,

"Do you think that we should be talking here?"

The adept looked with annoyance at the two foreigners, who spoke so casually during this vital ritual. He looked back to the master, who was preparing to shoot the next arrow.

"*Ni.*"

The adept only just caught the arrow and the assassin continued to talk to Acmed.

"It's fine, but what do you think of Zen and meditation?"

Acmed replied with a little thought and with a whisper in his voice, as the master shot again.

"*San.*"

"I believe meditation is a self-induced trance that allows you to connect with a primal state of the mind; the mind's natural state."

The assassin nodded as another arrow flew through the air.

"Good, most people do not understand trance states. Trance is neither esoteric nor mystical, it is low meditation."

The forth arrow shot and the old master spoke over them.

"*Shi.*"

"You see Acmed, even though this is low meditation, it still proves that anyone can meditate and that meditation is not an unachievable goal that needs years of work. It is years of work that help polish that meditation and make it more meaningful and deep."

Acmed nodded in understanding.

"So, master, would you say that meditation is a speciality of the east? Is it ingrained into the eastern mind and is it harder for the western brain to comprehend?"

The assassin smirked.

"Not at all, not at all. We have had meditation in the west as long as they have in the east. The power of prayer has been in our society and prayer is meditation, for meditation is nothing more then the quietening of the mind and concentration on a single point. Or you could say that it is the pursuit of a zero state of mind, a natural state of being."

Acmed questioned loudly and the old master shot and shouted at the same time,

"*Go.*"

Acmed's question continued over his voice and attack,

"So why are there hundreds of methods and countless books written on the subject of meditation?"

The adept caught the arrow but his eyes kept glaring at the rude visitors in his *Dojo*,

"You see Acmed, our nature is to classify; we pigeon-hole everything we can, in Latin and in Greek, in lists and tables. We like to order things. Once we have this order then we theorize it, it is this theorisation, with the want for recognition, that drives us to the plethora of documentation on a subject that is straightforward. However, even though simple in outline it is difficult to practise, difficult not because it is unnatural to us; it is in fact a natural state, but because we have surrounded ourselves with the unnatural, what is natural appears difficult. Our modern lives have driven us to live outside of the normal world around us, with self-made complexities that fight to give the conscious side of your mind domination over your thoughts. Once the conscious mind is chattering away, your zero mind or natural state is suppressed, thus unbalancing your mind. With an unbalanced mind it is harder to meditate as meditation is in fact the journey into a state of total relaxation, subconscious observation and self-maintenance. It is here that the point of our lesson arises."

"*Roku...Nana.*"

The old master shot two arrows consecutively; the adept caught both with an uneasy rush. The assassin continued, paying the ritual no heed, his voice rising in volume.

"You see, this self-maintenance and self reflection is what brings you to the correct decision. Without this time to reflect, your mind is following only the conscious rationalisation. Therefore as society is an imperfect construct around us that programmes us from birth, the mind is given to fault and the conscious thought process is corrupt with false information, corruption, fundamentalism, racism, political and power lusting. All of these factors plus the lack of ability to consult the subconscious realm results in the atrocities of the world. But let's now think of the other side: meditative reflection brings forth the elements of spirituality, questioning, humility and understanding. This reflective ability allows the two halves of your mind to temper each other, balancing out and allowing for proper decision making."

"*Hatchi.*"

The old master spoke in a whisper and waited for his shot.

"You see Acmed, it is a blend of cognitive thought, balanced emotion and a reflective mirror-like mind that shows true humanity."

Acmed interrupted,

"So would you say there are many true humans on the planet?"

The reply came along with the annoyed face of the adept.
"Indeed, young one, there are a minimal amount of real humans left. While mankind hits a population explosion, true humans are dying, leaving the world a world of zombies with no ability to reflect on their existence."
"*Kyu.*"
The arrow was caught with ease this time. Suddenly the assassin spoke in a much louder voice, continuing his conversation. The adept looked at him with a forced sideward's glance. The old master did not speak and simply realised an arrow. The adept moved with subconscious ease towards the trajectory of the projectile. At the same moment the assassin, in mid conversation, with a gentle flick of the wrist shot a blade at the adept. As he caught the arrow the assassin's knife, short and obsidian, stuck out of his throat. With black gargling blood the failed adept fell to his knees. The old master walked up to his fellow student and spoke in Japanese.
"An unbalanced mind."
The old man then moved over to the assassin and as the adept choked to death, spoke in broken English, "Thank you, master assassin."
Then with a bow the master began to leave. As he left, the assassin from his seated position bowed his head and spoke in perfect Japanese, "At your service."

XXVI
Science vs. religion

"Only god can give you a soul."
The placard was waving in the crowd, each of the others in this poster army had a similar message, each one directed at the cloning test station that the protesters were blockading. The assassin and Acmed were waiting for their target. They were waiting for the protest leader to open himself up for attack, to give them an opportunity to kill him.
"What do you think of cloning?"
Acmed placed the poison tipped needle back in its cap.
"I'm unsure about God so I don't really know. I suppose if God exists then he may be annoyed that we have gone too far but on the other hand, if he likes the progress we are making then he may see it in a different light. Then if God does not exist then no one will care and no harm has been done."
The assassin looked over the heads of the protesters, trying to find a way through, his speech broken by the bobbing of heads.
"For me cloning represents the constant argument between science and religion, a fruitless argument that benefits nobody but hinders all. For some reason religion hates the academic sciences for explaining the world around them and the scientists hate the religious for compounding mystery on what they need to be straight forward and plain. For me young Acmed it is a very simple thing, this argument is very simple indeed. God is God, no matter what name, he,

it, she, they, thing. God created the world if you have faith or belief in a god."

The assassin pointed to the world around him,

"You see by our being here we are proof of creation, we are the proof of the existence of creation. Science is simply a way to understand that creation, a way to look and explain. Religion first told us how to live, how to form ethics and to help understand our position. Science has now become a religion, a new religion that strives to go deeper into that creation."

The assassin and Acmed moved one line closer to the lead protester's position as the voices of the crowd became more and more heated. His face was red, fists raised in moral objection. The assassin continued.

"Science is fundamentally and continually wrong. From its dawn science has claimed to be correct, from the earth at the centre of the universe to the idea of the hunched unspoken Neanderthal, they have always been wrong. But it is being wrong that is the key to science, for science to progress it has to be fallible, it has to be wrong. For when an incorrect rule is made, it gives rise to a selection of questions, questions that don't fit into the ruling, thus we look deeper and harder and with this investigation we find further truth. It's not a whole truth but a simple small element of truth; this element is then added to our knowledge. When there are enough truthful elements to outweigh the falsehoods on the scales of reality, the rule we believed in is cast out and we have progressed, just a little."

With that last sentence the two assassins moved forward another line, slipping under the arms of the protesters. They slipped under a man who held his banner high; the banner read 'drenched in blood' and was splashed with red paint.

"And what of religion?"

The master assassin only just heard Acmed's question over the crowd.

"Religion...religion was the first science, but like all things it was codified and the beast of dogma took hold, a firm grip indeed. They no longer expanded on ethics and no longer searched for knowledge, they have what they believe is all they need, to understand the universe. All the great books are written by men. None of them have been physically handed to them by God, but these scriptures are taken as the word of the lord and as truths, truths based on the words of ancient man. It is here that religion fails. Here is why it is dying. They are bound by their own dogma. Their own words keep them from understanding. The ancient man who wrote those words would have sided with science, they would have wanted to see the exploration of knowledge. They would say the parables and stories are only to give the reader an understanding of higher concepts, to allow ethics to build. In some cases they are simply ancient man trying to understand how we came about, we know that the stories of first man and the creation myths are not true but they are sometimes a reflection of the reality of the big bang and the reality of evolution. They are attempts at religious mirror images to our arrival."

The crowd surged forward, the apprentice assassin reached for the poison needle but the master assassin stayed his hand.

"Wait, we won't reach."

The crowd pulled back and Acmed smiled at the master assassin's skill. The assassin spoke with a lower tone, trying not to be heard by the front row of the crowd.

"Science and religion are both wrong via their own egotism, their own self love. You see science and religion both have the view that they have the understanding, enough understanding to proclaim the secrets of the universe. You can liken this to an ant, the ant is sat on a leaf, the ant can see only so far. However as religion and science began to see into space and investigate the world on a microscopic level this 'ant' is now given a telescope to look out at the garden. With this new scope the ant, who could see only three leaves ahead of him, can now see ten leaves. Even though this knowledge has vastly improved his understanding of the field he is in, most of the world around him is still hidden. The meadow and the river next to him are totally obscure and the concept of the full shire is unthinkable. However the ant is now under the belief that he can postulate his surroundings from the knowledge he has acquired. He can imagine a universe and the possibility of a creating force. But you see Acmed from the point of view of a human the ant is stupid, it has no concept of its reality, it only understands a ten-leaf radius. The difference comes when that ant with its minimal knowledge postulates a doctrine and from this doctrine formulates and declares an absolute knowledge. So like the ant we have progressed but through our own egotism we have closed the doors of investigation and unity. If religion and science could only openly admit that they don't know everything and that they are not one hundred percent correct then they would unite and join into a crusade of knowledge to find the answers of the universe."

With a sudden surge the crowd moved forward, the assassin whispered.

"Now."

With fast reflexes Acmed slipped the top off the needle and as the crowd neared the protest leader the apprentice assassin pushed it into the fat of his leg. The protest leader flicked his hand at the annoyance then continued his speech. The assassin and the apprentice began to move away and people readily took their positions. As they walked away Acmed asked,

"So are you for or against cloning?"

The assassin smiled.

"Like the ant I don't have enough information to make a judgment, so in the true sense of this lesson, I would say – I don't know."

XXVII
THE SUPER NATURAL

"Things that go bump in the night."

The assassin smiled as he spoke, the two of them stood in the pale moonlight, underneath the church spire and surrounded by graves, each monolith casting its lunar shadow over the black-blue grass. The two of them were standing over a grave, a special grave; a grave that held the corpse of the assassin's master, and so the assassin spoke again.

"Things that go bump in the night, the shadow world, the supernatural, do you believe in the otherworld and its entities?"

The apprentice looked to the black spire, a doom-spike into heaven, then he looked to the grave.

"I have never come across anything of the spirit world, I have never had an encounter with another being or spirit, so as far as I can say, I do not know."

Acmed shrugged his shoulders and ended his sentence, the assassin smiled and looked pleased.

"Good answer boy, when one does not know, then one should say so. To admit that you have not the knowledge is a great step to being a true human. However, to get back to my topic, I do believe in the other world of the supernatural. I feel that even though the evidence for the supernatural is probably ninety percent false there is a good section that is hard to disprove. Coupled with the absence of absolute proof that it does not exist leads to only one conclusion, that is that it is real. However, we are not dealing with the logic of reality in this case."

The assassin smirked as he added the last sentence on. Acmed pondered as the church clock struck out the time, hollow bells on a misty evening. When the chimes had finished Acmed spoke.

"I disagree with your last sentence, I must add. I think that you are correct in the first point and I agree that it is probable that the supernatural exists but I disagree that it is outside of logic. The natural is what is contained in logic; the supernatural is what man cannot place within a scientific context. With that in mind the definition of supernatural changes depending on your chronological and geographical location. A tribesman of Africa or an ancient Celt would not have the scientific understanding that we have, therefore what we see as scientific they see as supernatural. With this in mind if we were to push ourselves into the future we may find that many of the things we hold as supernatural are in fact quite logical."

The assassin interrupted,

"Just because it is logical or if something has lost its mystery and you think it normal, does that mean it loses its mystic?"

The apprentice pondered in the still night.

"No. I truly believe that everything has an explanation and that all things have reason, but no matter how logical we make things, no matter how we label them, we live in a world of miracles, everyday miracles: babies are born, trees grow from seeds, the world holds a natural balance, the earth spins in an infinite void, the most colossal of miracles. However, we see these phenomena as normal, we label and explain the miracle but just because the miracle is explained does not make it any less marvellous. The world is full of the 'supernatural' but we have made it all 'natural'. So therefore, why should anything be impossible, science recognises multiple dimensions, a vast explosive universe and things that are quite incomprehensible to some. So why should anything be impossible, why is the thought of a supernatural dimension that occasionally crosses over to ours that impossible to understand?"

They both listened to the nightlife, a nocturnal orchestra that created a sweet symphony to those who took the time to listen. After a moment of thought Acmed spoke with a deep questioning.

"What then of those who claim connection with the spirit world?"

The assassin then gave his thoughts to the conversation,

"Well, Acmed, the connection between man and the other side is, I think, man made. Maybe it is possible that some people have this ability but I am not convinced. If there were people with this gift then they were proclaimed holy and were rewarded with 'wealth' of some form and where there is gold there are people who want it. Where there is a want that is bad enough they will then cheat for it. Tricksters and con artists, they became the possible downfall for the true belief in the spirit world, alongside the arrogance of science. So to summarise in this world of miracles and magic, we have found rationalizing through science. With this we have shown the con man to be false and have given over to the belief in the supernatural as a sign of ignorance. But what if you could take that all away, take away the science and the labels. You are left with a universe of miracles and explosive supernatural energy. So would it not be logical to think that some form of supernatural world, or set of 'beings' exist in our nature, a nature that we can not understand as of yet? It is more probable that mankind has not found the answer to the questions we ask. We all have some form of secret belief in something outside of the norm; we all fear the dark at some point. I think that man should open his mind and say 'I don't know'. He should accept that anything is possible in this and other dimensions. Science has radical theories about the reality of space and time, maybe just maybe we have not found our proof yet, and because of this we say it is all not true and we have given up the search for something 'supernatural'."

They both looked to the grave, a weird mist creeping in swirls, fingers of white outstretched, as though grasping from this world to the next. The apprentice spoke,

"The one thing I do disagree with is when a belief in the supernatural overcomes practicality, rationality, and human sense, when the religion of a people is based in the spiritual and they claim to converse with necromantic qualities. When this happens and decisions are made on human affairs by supposed communication between the dead and the living, it's a shame when the thin line of reality is cut."

The assassin smiled,

"True Acmed, true again this ignorance and the twisted concept of humans and their understanding of the world around them. People like that believe that they know, and once ignorance and tradition take hold then the death of rationality is born. Like people of the cloth and scientist these witchdoctors are lost, all it takes is for one of them to say 'we don't know' but we are on a journey of discovery, if this was said then life would take a new turn. Remember boy no matter how much knowledge you have gained you will never know it all, so always have a beginners mind, a blank sheet and if you do this you will be wise above all men."

Acmed sensed the change in the assassin's voice; he decided to leave his tutor at *his* master's grave. After Acmed had gone the assassin spoke solemn words, "Master, as you taught me, I still know nothing."

His form and the grave submerged into the mist.

XXVIII
DRUGS

Acmed and the assassin sat in a dimly lit area in a park that was notorious for its rough and violent nocturnal activities. Both master and apprentice were uncommonly dressed in hooded tops and ripped jeans, an uncultured change was had about their mannerisms and intonation with a distinctly different vocabulary, just for the occasion. A youth eyed them both up with caution and intrigue. The assassin gave an upwards nod and spoke with an inviting manner,
"You looking for something mate, you after a little exchange."
The youth spoke with slight shyness behind a cocky bravado,
"Yep, what you got?"
"What you into?" came the reply,
"Speed if you got it?"
"We have, how much?"
"A gram"
The assassin reached into his pocket and drew out a small brown packet; he tossed it to the boy,
"Check it out"
The youth picked up the envelope and tested its weight by tossing it several times in the air.
"How much?"
"For you its free, if you like it come back again and we will work out a price for more."
"Will do." came a nonchalant reply as he skulked off into the darkness.
Acmed questioned quietly,

"How long before he realises that the content of that packet has no drugs in whatsoever?"
The assassin smiled,
"Long after we have gone."
The assassin continued.
"Drugs have their place you know, their place in society. Ancient man used them to transcend consciousness, to open pathways in the mind, to explore other realities. They were used to find a heightened sense of reality, to open doors to 'other worlds'."
The assassin smirked as he spoke on,
"We know this through ethnographic research and archaeology but what we do not know is if those substances were abused and if the availability of drugs was a problem to ancient man or if he respected the experience. Of course the modern use is a depraved act of lack of self-control, a pure pleasure tool and route to a mental downfall. I myself have never taken drugs."
Acmed chirped in,
"Me neither."
The assassin talked past him,
"Modern drug taking is a sign of a weak character, a mind that has no substance, a mind lost in itself. Even the use of soft drugs and to an extent some legal substances such as tobacco and alcohol is a form of weakness. People cannot accept their position in life; they do not have the capacity to use their creativity and mental power to enrich their miserable lives. For this they turn to drugs to find an escape from the captivity of boredom they imprison themselves in."

Just then a pair of youths rounded the corner, a couple arm in arm, a skin headed man and a women with red sores around her lips. She spoke through those blisters,
"We hear that you are giving out samples."
The assassin took on his dealer's voice,
"True, you looking?"
"We are."
He took out two packets, past them to Acmed who swaggered over and handed them one each. The man looked at his and spoke with reflection in his voice.
"Be careful, there is a main dealer in this area, he will be round if he hears news of this."
"Thanks for the warning, we will look out."
As the couple retreated into the dark the master and apprentice continued.
"Acmed, the world has become a desperate place indeed when boredom is so much that one has to give in to such self-destructive urges like this. In such a world of wonder why would you need to?"
As the pair discussed the faults in the world of drugs, more and more people approached them as the word spread, more lost ghouls looking for a spike of escapism from their sad lives.
"Master, what would you do to solve the drugs problems in the world, how would you resolve this issue?"
A stern resolve came over the assassin,
"I would legalise all drugs."
Acmed raised his eyebrow and opened his mouth but before he could reply the assassin spoke,
"Wait Acmed, hear me out before you judge."
"Yes, master."

"First make a deal with all the drugs barons of the world, allow them to open legitimate companies and start a well structured and recorded distribution network. They would exchange guns for accountants and crime would fall being replaced by competitive business rivalry. Next you grow employment with production factories and quality control, decreasing unemployment. Then you install a high tax duty upon a clean drug allowing tax in other areas to drop, maybe replacing inheritance tax? Alongside this you would place warnings on each packet that anyone who uses drugs will be declined any medical help unless they have private health care. You see Acmed, there is one key issue here for my theory. I have met many drug abusers and every single person that I have met who does not take drugs said the same thing, every single one of them. Everyone who refused to take drugs said that they refused it, not because it was illegal, but because it was dangerous and stupid, the fact that it was illegal was not even an issue. So making drugs illegal does not decrease its user base, it simply increases crime. So the law is pointless, even dangerous as a law. If it was to be made legal there would be a spike in drug related deaths but as people realised the danger and watched friends die the lesson would hit home and so what if a few drug users died? There are too many people on the earth anyway, a few less uncreative zombies will do the world good, as harsh as it may sound. After the initial problems the system would right itself and all would be well. Now Acmed what did you have to say?"

Acmed smiled and raised his eyebrow,

"Nothing, its ok."
The assassin sat back and smiled inwardly,
"Well then would you like to hear the true solution for the drugs problem? It is for parents to take charge of their children's education, to instil morals and values to allow them to open their minds without aid."
"Fair comment." Acmed said.
"By the way what did you put in these packets?"
The assassin laughed,
"Laxatives and a vomiting solution. They may end up in hospital but they wont take drugs from strangers again, and the next time they take them they will wonder."
The assassin's sentence was interrupted by an angry shout,
"Oi, you!"
A thug with a bat and five friends.
"You are selling on my patch."
The assassin regained his true speech pattern and posture.
"You must be Hanson, I've been expecting you, there are certain high ranking police officials that have paid a lot of money for us to meet."
Hanson was taken back by this unexpected response but the assassin continued,
"You five may leave if you so wish, you have three seconds…1, 2…3, ok if you will."
Acmed and the assassin drew out long bladed knives and a bloody battle commenced a violent work of art.

XXIX
History

The vast enclaves of John Rylands library of Deansgate Manchester housed the assassin and his apprentice, alongside some of the world's best literary treasures. They sat in a reading area, each of them surrounded by glass-encased books.
"What do you think of Herodotus?"
The apprentice mimicked his master's whisper,
"The Greek father of history?"
"Yes, that one."
"He was the beginning of history as we know it."
"And, young one, what is history?"
"History is the biding that holds together identity, it is what makes us a unified people as opposed to simply self-functioning individuals."
The assassin smiled
"Good, good, that is it, and more."
The light beamed like honey and whiskey as it bathed the statue of Mrs Rylands the founder of this horde of treasure. The assassin sat back, framed by ancient treasures.
"History is the foundation of humanity. Before Herodotus, before the ancient scholars, were the bards, the keepers of knowledge, the campfire historians. These people kept the oral histories, the tales of the tribe, tales of creation and the heroes of old. This was a much-needed function in a world of mystery. This would place a human in context with his surroundings, give him an origin, thus creating a point that constitutes a start, and from this start he has a direction. Even though oral histories became

embellished, their function remains the same: to show direction, teach of mistakes and their solutions and inspire the next generation to greatness."

The assassin opened an archaic volume with his fingertips,

"Then came the written word and history gained a new function…power!"

The assassin's eyes flared and Acmed looked quizzical,

"Power?"

"Yes, once written down, a 'history' is factualized. Once supported it is a truth and truth is power. The Nazi party claimed authority through noble and original descent based on false archaeology. But the fact that it was false is irrelevant, in the eyes of millions it was a truth and the 'truth' gave rise to military power. Nations are bound together by their history, even if false. How many English people actually have native English blood? Most are Roman, Viking, French etc. But they are all bound by a history that is not connected to their blood. This false bond is a strong one indeed, it created the English identity, an identity that formed an empire, the largest in the world. An empire that both created and destroyed and even though now the empire has gone, we live in the bonds of its shadow and in the power of its history."

The assassin stood and asked Acmed to walk through the Neo-gothic vaults as he continued, "It's even more evident in America. Its history has created power and unified its people even though they know full well that is a 'false' unity and history. You see Acmed; to me 'white' Americans are simply

Europeans on a prolonged holiday. They all know that their ancestry is not American, its all from selected sections of Europe but still they now hold the world power because of the power they have through collected history. So you see, history is power, unified power is identity."

The two of them were in the panelled viewing rooms with oak and red velvet, looking at the delicate displays. The assassin spoke,

"There is something that amuses me, Acmed. We all love and give voice to our pride of our ancestry but there is an issue that most of us do not realise. While we all have a few traits in our culture that can be linked as an antecedent to the natives of our land we are in fact closer in culture to our modern foreign neighbours then we are to our historical blood line".

Acmed openly looked puzzled,

"You see, Acmed, if I visit most other countries today, even the most remote and underdeveloped, I would see a car; a man in a suit; a camera; a gun, a form of world wide religion; and I would probably know the name of the people, or they would have some English or there would be someone who could translate for me. On the other hand if I ventured into time, even in my own country I would find a world I did not know, a life so different that I could not comprehend it, even if I liked the style and the living better it would not be the culture I knew. The modern man would be closer to me, the person I call enemy would be more a brother then my head hunting Celt blood-father. So you see, world conflict through race and politics becomes ridiculous, we are now the same

culture, the same race, we just have hang-ups about archaic people we do not know or relate to."
Acmed dropped his shoulders and smiled,
"I see, and I do agree, it's quite shocking."
The assassin moved to the next cabinet, the light reflecting the Egyptian texts.
"Even though history has power, even though historically we are different from other cultures and even though we have professional historians, our history is wrong."
"Wrong?" Acmed voiced.
"Yes. Think – where does your history come from? Do you spend hours looking at current theories? Maybe, probably not. Most of your historical knowledge is not through school, or university, it is from the media, from films, documentaries, TV programmes, magazines, newspapers and alongside all these things is common held knowledge. All of these things are flawed; documentaries are researched by academics who wish to show their own theories; popular media is shallow, etc. but when I say wrong what I mean is that there is a part truth and lots of room for vast improvement. We all have but a glimpse of history, and that is all we have. True academics say that even though we have good theories and we have good educated guesses, we actually don't really know much for sure about history. Any academic who say that they are correct is false. Like the existence of God, we don't know, we only have beliefs. You may ask why it is so important to have 'correct' history. Well look at how some peoples are treated to genocide – a product of history gone wrong, twisted interpretations by people

who quest for dominance. Thus Acmed, the government funds a high percentage of research but a very low percentage of history of culture issues, they only see money as wealth. They create more technology that is being warped by evil people to injure more innocents and to persecute others based on a false history. We as a race must evolve spiritually, materially and genetically – so far we are obese, product-overusing robots devoid of spiritual force. To correct this we must study our history, with the purpose of learning from past mistakes, which will also place us in context within the evolution of man. It will give us a point of origin. In addition to this, history can give us the vision of what we should do in the future, a reality check of where we are and a trajectory to follow. We need to focus on a positive 'now' with an understanding of the past and a knowledge of the future."

Acmed and the assassin walked out in silence leaving the magnificence of John Ryland's library behind. Walking onto Deansgate, Acmed questioned,

"How long will it take him to die?"

"Not long."

XXX
Magic

"Do what thou will shall be the whole of the law."

An automatic response came from the crowd to a solemn command. Acmed and his master were in a dimly lit room, a room above a city centre bookshop, a book shop that sold instruction on the occult. Acmed looked around at the hooded figures in this *Thelemic* mass, hooked noses out of black cowls. The naked priestess sat on the alter and the priest, dressed in white, cloaked in crimson and crowned with a serpent, held aloft a gold rod. The assassin was seated far to the rear, treated as a high ranking honoured guest. His apprentice at his side, they spoke in almost inaudible voices as the mass continued. The assassin asked,

"Do you believe in magic?"

Acmed whispered back.

"No, no not at all, I thought I did once but now, no."

"That's a shame, for magic is truly the blood of hope…tell me what do you think magic is?"

Acmed paused for thought, the priestess raised her chalice, head uplifted.

"Well, magic by definition is the ability to control, manipulate and transform the physical world through means that defy logic and science."

"Very good, so you say that magic lies in the realm of the 'supernatural' or things that are external to logic?"

"Yes, that's about it." Acmed's whisper crept out.

"Ok, Acmed, let me now give an addition to your definition. I agree with you except for the fact that magic is outside of our logic. Now ancient man believed and accepted magic, it was within his logical infrastructure. I feel that magic is the ability to control, manipulate and transform the world around us with the power of the mind, an untapped power that we all have. Let me clarify further, Acmed, before your eyebrows come off the top of your head. Science agrees that hypnosis exists and works. We have an agreement that the aura exists, we have ample proof for telekinesis, so called 'poltergeist' attacks, mesmerism. The scientific world accepts trance as a state of consciousness, dowsing, lay lines and all the other countless things that were held as esoteric and on the edge of logic, things that are now under the umbrella of acceptance and understanding. These things have come into our logic, even if they are on the periphery, therefore they are no longer magic. To a god all things are logic, humankind has floated between these two points, backwards and forwards depending on the understanding of the people at each time, somewhere between ignorance and infinite logical understanding. I truly think that we, as a race have gone back in time and understanding in comparison to some of our ancestors."

The priest dipped his wooden staff in the priestesses bronze chalice, the simulated the vocal expression of an orgasm as a wafer was dropped into some wine. Acmed lent over in the treacle light.

"But do you not think that ancient man was deceived or outwitted by charlatans?"

The assassin smiled a menacing grin

"Well, let me say this first, if the occult is real, then only a fraction of the practitioners are real or true, a vast percentage are tricksters and money-makers, conmen and vagabonds. The rest are powerless people who search for magical power in varying degrees of earnest. I think that this has been the truth in all times of human existence from the cave, to the grave of man."

"Now to answer your question, ancient man built Stonehenge, the Pyramids, invented geometry, mathematics, engineering, philosophy, physics. All of this came about not in our time but the time of magic, we simply use their knowledge to create technology, we don't expand ourselves that much. Even though they knew all of these things they held magic in a high regard, this leaves me with the conclusion that the use of the mind as a physical manipulator was possibly a reality that has been cut off in our modern surroundings. Scientists agree that there are vast amounts of areas in the brain that are untapped, areas we are unsure of. If we could harness the possible power that lies in these deep sections maybe we can affect the world around us, by non conventional means, or as some would say - magic."

The assassin's face disappeared into shadow as he spoke, the mass was climaxing and the audience started to queue up for a pagan communion. Each one in turn stood at the front of the alter, arms crossed, a wafer and wine in each hand and in turn each person declared,

"There is no part of me that is not of the gods."

Acmed whispered as the procession ended,

"So you are saying that all is magical and more importantly that it may be possible that people have areas of the brain that we can strengthen and use to interact with the world around us, interact in a way that would defy logical understanding…maybe?"

"I don't know but I think it is a rational understanding and one that would best fit in with the limits of our logic."

Acmed watched as the silence of the last member finished their declaration and the priest spoke and the priestess waited behind a veil.

"Master, thus you have given me speculation; we have had idol chat but no real lesson, what's your motive?"

The assassins face came into view

"Good, good the point, well the point is this. As always we do not know, can we tap energy in our brain, we simply do not know but what I do know is that modern living is driving away the esoteric, the experimental we are locking areas of our mind that were once open, telepathy, pre-cognition, intuition, simple gut feeling and awareness, these things are dying. So my lesson is this, take time from moneymaking, merriment and accumulation. Take a small section of time to explore its mind, if man can use 5% of his brain imagine what he could do with 100%, its said that man was created in the image of God, if we can perfect our minds maybe we can achieve what is at the moment logically impossible."

The assassin was interrupted by fits of horrific bloody coughing- the mass was in uproar blood and bile filled the floor, alters other-thrown and the dying all the around. Acmed accustomed to death sat back and watched,

"Why master?"

"I was once a member of the *Ordo Templi Orientis* or O.T.O. I thought I was on a journey of learning but my brother members and peers used free thinking and mental progression to disguise the dogma or folly of their closed minds. I don't mind ignorant people but I hate open-mindedness and awareness that transmutes into a blockade of evolution and a stand for hypocrisy. In this world we must all stand on a stone above the crowd and see with a free vision, not stand on the stone blindfolded."

From the back came a figure holding the wine.

"It's done, brother assassin."

The assassin knocked on the arm of his chair, first three times then five knocks then three more.

"93 deaths."

XXXI
Reincarnation

"Do you think that he will be reincarnated?"
"Who?" Acmed frowned
"The body at your feet, the one you just killed?"
Acmed wiped his face clean with a knife-clenched fist, leaving strips of blood.
"Yes, sorry, I see what you mean…him."
"Good Acmed, you are learning to accept death with ease, seeing it as a means to an end and not the end itself, but my question still stands, do you think he will be reincarnated?"
Acmed chuckled
"What you mean is do I believe in reincarnation and can I learn a lesson from this, even if I do or do not have that belief?"
"Good, good, marvellous, you are becoming a true human; you are seeing the truth, I'm proud."
The two dressed in blue overalls and sprayed in blood stood looking at each other with intent. The assassin spoke first,
"My question?"
"Do I believe in reincarnation, I understand it is the concept that is deep in the minds of millions of people it is ancient and prolific, the notion of multiple existences that occur to the same 'soul' until that soul has understood the lessons needed and advanced enough to proceed to 'heaven', do I believe in this?"
The assassin waited for Acmed to continue
"Well I do know that the big questions in life go unanswered and we have no proof so all I can give you is my belief. I don't know if I do have any faith

in this phenomenon but what I do know is that there are people of intellect that say they have been reincarnated and millions of people believe in it. Plus there is nothing to say that the concept of going to heaven or another such place or even simply ending your existence is more correct the anything else. So yes I believe in the possibility of the idea of reincarnation."

Acmed picked up a saw and began to saw through the legs of the body at his feet. The assassin followed suit and picked up his saw, concentrating on the neck.

"So, apprentice, what does that tell you about reincarnation?"

Acmed talked over the violent sawing motions,

"Well as I said I know nothing of reincarnation itself but we can work something out from it. Reincarnation or the theory of reincarnation has nothing to do with the after life, its all to do with the here and now."

Blood sprayed over his mouth as he spoke,

"It instils fear, fear of coming back to earth as something worse then what you are now, it tells you that living a bad life will Bring you back in a worse position then what you are in. but equally it also rewards if you do well you come back better off. Therefore reincarnation is to reinforce an ethical code, it's to ensure that you live well, it is a safety guide for society."

The assassin pulled the head clear of the body

"Very good young one, very good, anything more?"

Acmed pulled off the lower leg with a snap of the final tendon and placed it in the bag next to the victim."

"Yes there is always the three-fold mythology, the fact that if you do something bad then it will revisit you three times worse and if you do good you will receive thrice the reward."
The assassin started on the arms
"Do you think that that is true?"
Acmed spat out some blood,
"I do but I don't know if its divine judgment, maybe it is and maybe it is not but what I do know is this. If you are a good to people and when I say good, I mean good for no personal gain then people will start to like you more, as they do they think positively about you, when that happens people are nice around you and generally fill your encounters with a good feeling. In turn you feel stronger and you should achieve more and have a better existence. On the other hand if you are a negative or nasty person then you will be a magnet for negative responses and you will start a landslide of negativity towards you."
The assassin put both arms in the bag,
"I'm glad you said goodness without reward, this is the key to good ethics. If you give with hidden ambition then no matter how deep you hide it the person you are helping will pick up on it and the blight of negativity will be on you, it is the maggot inside the golden apple. Even if you set out with the idea doing good things for the benefit of feeling good you will only fail. You must do good deeds for the pure joy of helping others, if you can resign yourself to helping with no want for reward then you will benefit in the end."
The two assassins set to work on the torso. Acmed listened as his master continued his speech.

"But there is more, people expect to get results soon, but this is folly. The time frame for the benefit of good deeds is a long one and not fixed. If you are generally unliked then it takes a long time for people's opinions to change. It could take years and the slog is hard. If you have a negative reputation then your work is cut out for you. If you start with a good reputation then logically you will not take as long as the others to gain the benefits of your work. But this is irrelevant you should just stop now! Change now and be nice and try to do well in all situations, at all times live by this simple philosophy and your life will be like a wonderful dream, full of friends and positivity. But its hard, you must throw away all egotism. Care not for personal want and give your most valuable asset away - time."

They put all the parts into the bag and began to mop up.

"Lastly Acmed, you must not be made a fool of, don't let people take advantage of you, get those people out of your life, attach yourself only to the positive thinkers."

The two had changed and prepared to leave, clean and unnoticed.

"Acmed, remember reincarnation is not about after – it's about living well now."

XXXII
Failure

The assassin was looking through the scope of a high-powered rifle. The view in the sight was of Her Majesty's misty submarine dockyard at HMS Dolphin. The assassin was aiming at an officer on the top of the submarine conning tower, a distinct English gentleman and officer. Even if he was a bit young his posture was formidable. The two assassins were in a section of the dockyard rafters, dark and hidden, heavy in the shadow. Acmed whispered,
"Is the shot ok?"
"The shot's fine. I just have a feeling that something is wrong. There is something too powerful about that officer."
 At that very second, a thin line of wire dropped from the shadows above them and hooked itself perfectly over the assassin's head and onto his neck. With a terrible click a weight fell from the rafters above and the line tightened with unimaginable velocity. The assassin tried to vomit without passage as the weight of his body was dragged upwards. Acmed with trained reflexes jumped to his feet and reached for his master. As he did this the officer on the submarine far in the distance reached down and picked up a high-powered rifle of his own. Within seconds the rifle was shouldered and cocked ready for firing. Then it hit, a sonic slug, a fist of lead crashed through Acmed's skull, bone and flesh evaporated into a maelstrom of red mist. As Acmed's dead body fell from its perch the Master assassin's life was dancing

the Tyburn jig of the hanging dead. With a last effort the assassin's body went limp, master and assassin dead.

The officer from the submarine arrived at the dockyard, a slender powerful man with Icelandic blonde hair stood under the rafters. He called up,
"Master, are you there?"
A black rope descended from the heavenly shadows and a figure rigged in gloomy grey slid down until he reached the ground. This time an older man, a Master assassin, also with short cropped Icelandic blonde hair and threatening blue eyes. The master spoke,
"Come Dryce sit with me a moment, I wish to reflect with you."
"Of course my master, as you wish."
The two sat down and the Master assassin spoke in English with a heavy accent.
"Young Dryce, today is a day to be marked in the halls. It is a glorious yet terrible day. Today I have vanquished my old archenemy and his apprentice but it is tragic because he was a man of formidable stature, a true human. The world is a worse place for his passing and I shall lament as well as rejoice. But we must take something from this tragic loss to the world, we must learn a lesson."
Dryce sat back in the classic pose he adopted when he knew his master would give voice to his thoughts. He sat and listened; glad he was the only apprentice to this vast and dignified killer.
"Today we have witnessed failure, and failure is ever present in our lives. Failure is as certain as death; no single person can go through life without knocking

on the door of the despair of not succeeding. My old friend and enemy here at my feet is at the door of ultimate failure and he has paid the price of his life for my success. But failure rarely results in death; usually it results in a list of problems that appear. So as humans we must prepare ourselves for failure and its costs. Most people when they fail take it as a personal affront to their abilities and dwell on the limitations of their character. These failures build up and amass and transform themselves into a complex. This stain on our minds stops us from trying further; it stops our creativity and our enthusiasm."

The Master assassin paused looking for the foreign words.

"There are a few reasons why people fail, and you have to identify why you have failed in your own heart. Firstly, there is lack of ability; people attempt things that are far outside their capabilities, they have dreams that are unrealistic to their social position, financial ability and natural aptitude. The main concern here is the natural aptitude, for money and social standing are achievable, a lack of natural ability is fatal to any programme you undertake. Secondly, people fail because they only see the end goal as a target and reach for it prematurely. You must see that some goals are far outside your reach but not your ability. If you have the ability but not the reach then you should find stepping stones to your ambitions; you should identify the path that your reach can cover and then, like a mountain climber get to the top in small steps. But be warned, don't stop at the bottom and spend all your time wishing to be at the top. You have to make small steps, but you must keep making them. Lastly, there is divine intervention; there are just some things that you cannot do. There are people who have the ability and they have the reach and the charisma to do these things. But for some reason they don't seem to succeed; fate turns them bad luck at all corners and there appears to be powers working against them. If you know in your heart you have the ability and the reach but life keeps pushing you away from your goal then you must find a way around the fates or else accept it and put your view on another target, maybe in the direction that your fate is flowing."

The Master assassin looked at the bodies on the floor, draped in blood and not long out of life's love. He stood up and walked over to them both. He searched them until he found what he was looking for; each figure had a handmade pattern-wielded dagger. He weighed them in his hand and said,

"We must bury these knives of the order and dedicate these warriors to the mighty Odin. May Odin grant them war and glory in the halls of Valhalla."

Having retrieved the scarred blades that each assassin of the order carries, the Master assassin sat down and spoke again to his apprentice.

"Failure makes or breaks a man. If you fail and you take it as experience and carry that experience on you will be a tempered blade of a human. If you take all defeat as a personal affront to your abilities, it will act as a rot, infesting your soul, breaking you down from the inside out. If you let failure chip away at your spirit you will die a hollow and weak carcass as opposed to a strong and flexible light. Odin's wrath to any man who lets life defeat him!"

The Master assassin took one of the knives and set to work on removing the fingertips from each hand on the two slain corpses. They shall remain nameless in the eyes of the law. The assassin and his apprentice Dryce began to walk off, giving one last wend to their fallen enemies, enemies who had failed but died as true men. As they walked away along the misty dockyard the Master assassin finished his lesson.
"Dryce, you must realise one main thing where failure is concerned. You must understand that if I was confronted with a choice of two men I would give respect to just one of them. Better is the poor man who has tried all his life, he has failed countless times and still remains poor. It is better that he sacrificed his house, his land and his wealth on a failed dream. He is a better man then the poor man who says that he could have tried and if he did try he would have done better, he could have been a king, he could have had a fine life. Woe to that man who claims this for if he did not try then a weak man he is. True life is found in a list of failures as opposed to a list of wishes. It is failure that drives a man to succeed. If you understand that you have failed then you have nothing to lose. A man with nothing to lose is a man at the beginning of his dreams.

About the Author

Antony John Cummins MA of the most, noble city of Manchester on those haunted shores of England has a degree in Ancient History and Archaeology and a Masters Degree in Archaeology, both of which were obtained at The Victoria University of Manchester. Antony is a published author, artist and illustrator and still needs a day job. However, he has; lived and trained in Japan, also lived with the *Tongo* people of Ghana, Africa, sailed the high seas on tall-ships, racing those dignified draughts around Norway and France, and generally enjoyed life to the full.

On controlling urges.
Eating
Smoking
Releasing sexual tension
↓
    All emotions, urges, energies not quelled until satisfied.

Possible to be more energetic in a constant state of want?

Yes, especially sexual desire (energy) when you're horny you're distracted but arguably more aware of the fact you are alive.

A way to control it, And have clarity of mind?

Certainly deserves more than a cursory glance...

Printed in the United Kingdom
by Lightning Source UK Ltd.
134741UK00001B/48/P